The Age of Diminished Expectations

The Age of Diminished Expectations

U.S. Economic Policy in the 1990s

third edition

Paul Krugman

The MIT Press
Cambridge, Massachusetts
London, England

The Age of Diminished Expectations was first published in 1990 by the Washington Post Company as the first book in their series *Briefing Books*.

Third Printing, 1997

This book was set in Palatino by The MIT Press and was printed and bound in the United States of America.

Library of Congress Cataloging-in-Publication Data

Krugman, Paul R.
  The age of diminished expectations: U.S. economic policy in the 1990s / Paul Krugman.
    p.   cm
  Includes index.
  ISBN 0-262-11181-0 (hc). ISBN 0-262-61092-2 (pbk)
  1. United States –Economic policy–1981-   2. Economic forecasting–United States.
I. Title.
HC106.8.K78 1993
338.973'009'049–dc20
                                                            93-6411
                                                              CIP

Contents

Foreword

Today economic writing is better than ever it used to be. But now there is so much of it—often arguing at cross-purposes—that you as an intelligent and motivated reader are more up in the air than ever. What to do?

Needed is a competent guide, prepared by a tested and proved researcher, a briefing book to select the essentials for emphasis and sort them out in a good-sense way that will earn your confidence and understanding. That is a tall order. But Paul Krugman is the economist to try to do the job. And I see that he has succeeded wonderfully well.

I am proud of my generation of policy economists. You know their names: Walter Heller, Milton Friedman, John Kenneth Galbraith, Arthur Okun, Herbert Stein, Peter Drucker, and many more. But, as some sage has said, science progresses funeral by funeral. Paul Krugman is the rising star of this century and the next, and the world beats a path to his door. International finance is his thing, but that is only one of the many strings to his fiddle. The World Bank, the IMF, the Bank of Japan, and the Boston Fed—all seek to tap his fountain of wisdom and new ideas.

The Age of Diminished Expectations is a tour de force. To economists and noneconomists using it as a chart to navigate through the mysteries of inflation and recession, supply-side economics and productivity, floating exchange rates and bouncing stock markets, I say *Bon Voyage!*

Paul A. Samuelson
May 1990

Preface

There are three kinds of writing in economics: Greek-letter, up-and-down, and airport.

Greek-letter writing—formal, theoretical, mathematical—is how professors communicate. Like any academic field, economics has its fair share of hacks and phonies, who use complicated language to hide the banality of their ideas; it also contains profound thinkers, who use the specialized language of the discipline as an efficient way to express deep insights. For anyone without graduate training in economics, however, even the best Greek-letter writing is completely impenetrable. (A reviewer for the *Village Voice* had the misfortune to encounter some of my own Greek-letter work; he found "equations, charts, and graphs of stunning obscurity . . . a language that makes medieval scholasticism seem accessible, even joyous.")

Up-and-down economics is what one encounters on the business pages of newspapers, or for that matter on TV. It is preoccupied with the latest news and the latest numbers, hence its name: "According to the latest statistics, housing starts are up, indicating unexpected strength in the economy. Bond prices fell on the news . . . " This kind of economics has a reputation for being stupefyingly boring, a reputation that is almost entirely justified. There is an art to doing it well—there is a Zen of everything, even short-term economic forecasting. But it is unfortunate that most people think that up-and-down economics is what economists do.

Finally, airport economics is the language of economics bestsellers. These books are most prominently displayed at airport bookstores, where the delayed business traveler is likely to buy them. Most of these books predict disaster: a new great depression, the evisceration of our economy by Japanese multinationals, the collapse of our money. A minority have the opposite view, a boundless optimism: new technology or supply-side economics is about to lead us into an era of unprecedented economic progress. Whether pessimistic or optimistic, airport economics is usually fun, rarely well informed, and never serious.

But what is there for the intelligent reader who wants to be well informed but doesn't want to study for a Ph.D.? The answer, unfortunately, is not much.

In 1989 the *Washington Post* approached me with the idea of writing a short book about the U.S. economy that would be accessible to a nonprofessional public while maintaining intellectual quality. They envisioned this as a pilot for a series of briefing books on a variety of issues, from national defense to the environment, where the specialists and the educated public had ceased to speak a mutually intelligible language. This book is the result.

The title of the book, and its theme, came to me when I tried to put my finger on what airport economics gets wrong. The most important problem with the books at the newsstand, it seemed to me, is that they allow no middle ground between disaster and bliss. Either the economy is about to disintegrate or things will be wonderful—and since the economy rarely disintegrates, those people who are not in a doom-and-gloom mood will usually conclude that we are doing fine. Yet avoiding crisis and doing well are not the same thing.

The simple fact is that the U.S. economy is not doing well, compared with any previous expectation. In the late 1960s, nearly everyone expected the great postwar boom to continue. *Fortune*, for example, predicted in 1967 that real wages would increase by 150 percent by the year 2000. In fact, real wages are no higher now than they were at the time of the article. While a few Americans have prospered to an unprecedented extent, poverty in America has been increasing in both extent and severity.

When will all these disappointments come to a head? Quite possibly never—which is why airport economics is so misleading. One can have stability without progress, avoid a depression without achieving solid economic growth. That has been the story of the U.S. economy for the past generation, and will probably be its story for some time to come.

One might have expected that America's economic problems would come to a head in another way, through the political process. Relative to what almost everyone expected a generation ago, our economy has done terribly; surely one would have expected a drastic political reaction. Yet despite the occasional flurry of populism, such a backlash has never arrived. I find the lack of protest over our basically dreary economic record the most remarkable fact about America today. Whether it is a sign of our political strength or weakness, it is astonishing how readily Americans have scaled down their expectations in line with their performance, to such an extent that from a political point of view our economic management appears to be a huge success.

This, then, is my theme. We live in an "age of diminished expectations," an era in which our economy has not delivered very much but in which there is little political demand that it do better. In this book I try to document both our economic failures and our successes. More important, I try to explain *why* we are not making more of an effort to do something about our disappointing economy—which comes down in large part to the painfulness of the measures that we would have to take if we were serious about making a difference. And I try to chart the eventual consequences of continuing our present policy.

Along the way this book tries to convey a number of things that professional economists know but that the broader public generally does not. It is important to understand why inflation is less costly to endure and more costly to stop than most people realize; why protectionism, while usually a bad thing, does not cause depressions; how the savings-and-loan debacle was created by misplaced free-market rhetoric. On these and other issues I have found that the simple truth is widely regarded as shocking and heretical.

I hope that America will eventually be roused from its slumber and once again begin to face up to problems instead of letting them slide. The beginning of action must, however, lie in understanding. This book is not a political tract or a call to arms. It is something rarer: an attempt to describe the way things are, and explain why.

Introduction

It is hard nowadays to imagine what it must have been like to be a real optimist about the economy—to believe, as most Americans did a generation ago, that things could only get better, that individuals could count on steadily rising incomes and parents could confidently expect their children to move up in the world. It would be wrong to say that Americans have become economic pessimists; despite occasional bouts of anxiety over unemployment and corporate downsizing, most people continue to find their economic situation tolerable and their prospects acceptable. But high hopes have been replaced by, at best, stoic acceptance.

In at least one important respect the U.S. economy has continued to perform pretty well: there are still jobs for the great majority of people who want them. There was a prolonged job slump in the early 1990s, but even at its worst in the summer of 1992 the unemployment rate reached only 7.7 percent—nothing like the 10.7 percent that prevailed at the bottom of the previous slump in 1982. By the summer of 1996 the unemployment rate was back down to 5.3 percent, close to a 20-year low. And the economic recovery had added more than 10 million jobs.

While providing jobs is no small achievement, it is not the same as providing solid prosperity. Even during periods of economic expansion, like the 1992–96 recovery, the U.S. economy no longer delivers the kind of unambiguous economic progress that previous generations took for granted. Although some people have become fabulously rich, and a fraction of the population has achieved unprecedented affluence, the typical American family and the typical American worker earn little more today than they did 20 years ago. Indeed, for the median American worker there has been no increase in real take-home pay since the first inauguration of Richard Nixon. And for Americans in the bottom fifth of the income distribution, the years since 1980 have been little short of nightmarish, with real incomes dropping, the fraction of the population in poverty rising, and homelessness soaring.

There are, of course, bright aspects to the picture. One is the success of the economy at generating jobs, absorbing the baby boom and the massive movement of women into the paid labor force without a bulge in unemployment. Inflation, which seemed out of control in the 1970s, has subsided to a level that generates little discomfort. The huge trade deficits that frightened many observers in the mid-1980s have not gone away, but strong export growth has kept them of manageable size relative to the economy —and U.S. producers have regained market share in some industries, like automobiles, that had become symbols of national decline.The U.S. economy is not without strengths.

Yet overall our economy has done far worse over the past generation than anyone would have predicted. We have entered an era in which economic progress has become a doubtful thing. Many Americans feel that they live worse than their parents; even more fear that their children will be worse off than themselves.

In the first edition of this book I coined a name for this new era: the age of diminished expectations. The name has caught on, and is now widely used even by people who didn't read my book.

Although Americans now freely admit that something has gone wrong, there is still great confusion about what the problem is, even among those who try to follow public affairs. Many concerned people are convinced that our difficulties are primarily financial, and could be cured if only the budget deficit could be eliminated. Others are convinced that our problem is essentially one of international competition, from Japan and/or the Third World. There are even a few die-hard supply-siders, who think that if only George Bush had been more like Ronald Reagan the boom years from 1982 to 1989 might have gone on forever.

What even the would-be informed public seems to lack is a sense of how the various policy issues that fill the newspapers and talk shows fit together. During the 1992 campaign Ross Perot promised to fix the economy by "raising the hood and getting to work on it"; but woe to the auto mechanic who starts poking around without a good idea of how a car works! What do the budget deficit and health care costs have to do with the international competitive position of U.S. manufacturing? What does that competitive position have to do with real wages and income distribution? Not many people have a good sense of the answers to these questions, and many who think they know the answers have them wrong.

Unlike most books written about our economy, then, this book is not a work of advocacy. It is, instead, a guidebook to the economic landscape. Or if you prefer Ross Perot's metaphor, it is an owner's manual for our sputtering economic engine. It attempts, in as plain an English as possible, to explain how things fit together. It will not push for particular answers to our problems, although it will be obvious as we go along that some proposed answers are silly while other have promise (and that some problems have no easy answers).

The book is divided into five parts. The first part addresses the overall economic landscape: the trends that have had the biggest impact on the well-being of large numbers of Americans. A clear view of these trends is important if we want to know how well the economy is doing—but they are not policy issues right now

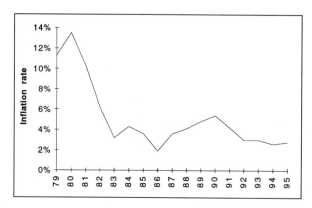

Figure 1
Inflation declined after 1980. . .

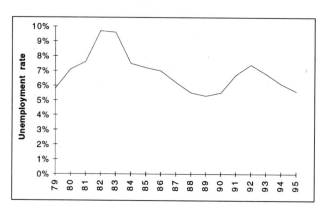

Figure 2
. . .and unemployment remained relatively low after its 1982 peak.

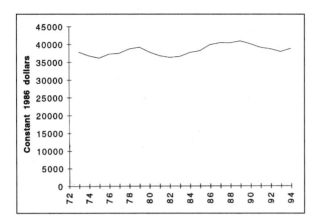

Figure 3
But the real income of typical families stagnated. . .

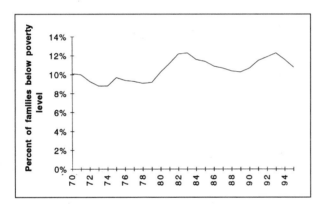

Figure 4
. . .and many more people were in poverty in the early 1990s than in the 1970s.

because no seriously debated policy changes would affect them very much.

The second part turns to two aspects of the economy that are widely regarded as problems, and that our government could resolve if it really wanted to: the trade deficit and inflation. As will become clear, however, the government in fact has balked at doing anything significant to reduce either the trade deficit or the rate of inflation—and in this age of diminished expectations, that lack of action has proved acceptable to the public, so long as no crisis results.

The third part of the book discusses a series of narrower policy issues, all interrelated: the budget deficit, health care, monetary policy, the dollar, protectionism and U.S.-Japan relations. All of these issues bear on, and are colored by, concerns about trade and inflation.

No picture of the American economy in the 1990s would be complete without some mention of the extraordinary events that have taken place in the financial markets. The fourth part of the book describes three "financial follies": the savings and loan crisis, the depredations of rogue traders, and the mysteries of international money.

The book ends with a discussion of America's prospects: What is likely to go wrong (or right) with the U.S. economy? Will the policy sins of the past meet retribution in the future? Will we on the contrary experience a renewed prosperity that makes the doomsayers seem foolish? Or will we simply drift along as we have, neither doing well nor experiencing a crisis?

I

The Roots of Economic Welfare

The well-being of the economy is a lot like the well-being of an individual. My happiness depends almost entirely on a few important things, like work, love, and health, and everything else is not really worth worrying about—except that I usually can't or won't do anything to change the basic structure of my life, and so I worry about small things, like the state of my basement. For the economy, the important things—the things that affect the standard of living of large numbers of people—are productivity, income distribution, and unemployment. If these things are satisfactory, not much else can go wrong, while if they are not, nothing can go right. Yet very little of the business of economic policy is concerned with these big trends.

To many readers this list may seem too short. What about inflation or international competitiveness? What about the state of the financial markets or the budget deficit? The answer is that these problems are in a different class, mainly because they have only an indirect bearing on the nation's well-being. For example, inflation (at least at rates the United States has experienced) does little direct harm. The only reason to be concerned about it is the possibility—which is surprisingly uncertain—that it indirectly compromises productivity growth. Similarly, the budget deficit is not a problem in and of itself; we care about it because we suspect that it leads to low national saving, which ultimately leads to low productivity growth.

So it is important to start our tour of the economy with the right perspective, which is that only the big three issues really matter very much. It is also important to be aware that on two out of the three big issues the American economy has not been performing at all well. Unfortunately, as we review the state of play on these big issues, we will also see that nobody is likely to do much about them.

1   Productivity Growth

Productivity isn't everything, but in the long run it is almost everything. A country's ability to improve its standard of living over time depends almost entirely on its ability to raise its output per worker. World War II veterans came home to an economy that doubled its productivity over the next 25 years; as a result, they found themselves achieving living standards their parents had never imagined. Vietnam veterans came home to an economy that raised its productivity less than 10 percent in 15 years; as a result, they found themselves living no better—and in many cases worse—than their parents.

Although the overwhelming importance of productivity should be obvious, not everyone understands it—or worse, they think that productivity is important for the wrong reasons, such as to help our international competitiveness. So it is worth spending a little while thinking about the issue.

As a starting point, it might be useful to think about how productivity and living standards would be related if the United States did not have any foreign trade. This may seem an outrageous omission, since many people think that productivity is important precisely because we need to be productive to compete on world markets. But this isn't really right—and imagining an economy without trade is a good way to see why.

Suppose, then, that the U.S. economy had no foreign trade so that everything we consume had to be made here. (Incidentally, this isn't such a bad approximation to reality. Even in 1996, with a more integrated world economy than ever before, about 87 percent of the goods and services we consume in the United States will be produced here.) How could we raise our consumption per capita? As a matter of pure arithmetic, there are only three ways:

(i) We could increase our productivity so that each worker produces more.

(ii) We could put a larger portion of the population to work.

(iii) We could put a smaller fraction of our output aside as investment for the future and devote more of our productive capacity to manufacturing goods for current consumption.

Obviously, (iii) is not a long-term way to increase consumption: We can consume more for a while by investing less, but that will surely cut into our ability to consume later. Option (ii) can work for a while if a substantial fraction of the population is unemployed, or if social change brings new groups into the work force; thus rapid growth in the share of the population employed took place as America emerged from the Depression, and again in the 1970s as women entered the work force in large numbers. But over the long term there are evident limits on this: You can increase the share of the population employed from 57 to 62 percent, as we did in the 1970s and 1980s, but you can't increase it to 105 percent.

So the only way in which sustained, long-term growth in living standards can be achieved is by raising productivity. Real consumption per capita in the United States today is about four times what it was at the turn of the century; so is productivity.

Now let's put foreign trade back into the picture. As a trading economy the United States sends part of its output abroad as exports, while importing part of what its people consume. If we can somehow manage to import more without having to export more as well, we can also increase our consumption. This therefore adds two more ways in which per capita consumption can rise:

(iv) We can import more without selling more abroad—which means that we have to borrow or sell assets to pay for the extra imports.

(v) We can get a better price for our exports so that we can afford to import more without borrowing.

Obviously (iv), like (ii), is an option for the short term only, since eventually the borrowing needs to be repaid. As for (v), the problem is how to persuade foreigners to pay more for our goods. The only reliable way to do that is to make our goods better—which is really just a productivity increase under another name.

So the essential arithmetic says that long-term growth in living standards—like the doubling of our standard of living in the generation following World War II, or the tenfold increase in

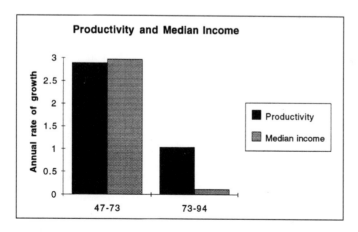

Figure 5
The stagnation of real family incomes during the 1970s and 1980s, like the soaring incomes of the previous generation, was driven by trends in productivity. The doubling of productivity from World War II to 1973 also doubled real incomes; the stagnation of productivity since then has held family incomes down.

Productivity and competitiveness

Many people believe that the most important reason why productivity growth is essential to the U.S. economy is to allow us to compete in the world economy. This is a misconception: productivity growth is no more (and no less) important in an economy open to international trade than in a closed economy.

To see why, it's useful to carry out a thought experiment. First, imagine a world in which productivity in all countries, including the United States, rises at 1 percent per year. What would be the trend in our standard of living? Most people have no difficulty in agreeing that living standards in all countries will rise by 1 percent annually.

Now suppose that productivity growth in the rest of the world rises to 3 percent, while it stays at 1 percent here. Now what is the trend in our living standards? Many people automatically answer that our living standards will stagnate or even decline, because we will have trouble competing. But they're wrong.

The right answer is that our real income will still grow about 1 percent per year. After all, why do we care about productivity growth abroad? It matters only if it affects the quantity of imported goods we receive per unit of goods that we export, that is, the price of our exports relative to the price of our imports (known as our terms of trade). And productivity growth abroad need not hurt our terms of trade—it is equally likely to improve them. There are several ways to see this. One is to note that while growth abroad increases the competition we face, it also expands our overseas markets. Another is to realize that when foreign firms whose products compete with our exports become more productive, those who provide us with imports generally also become more productive. Yet another way to see the point is to realize that faster productivity growth in foreign industries that compete with our exports will generally be reflected in higher wage growth as well, which can more than wipe out any relative cost gain. (These are all different ways of looking at the same story.)

In principle, then, the fact that our productivity growth lags behind growth abroad need not pose a problem. What about in practice? The actual U.S. terms of trade (excluding oil and farm products, which are subject to erratic movements) declined 15 percent from 1970 to 1980, and a further 2 percent from 1980 to 1991. These are very small numbers: since non-oil imports are only 7 percent of GDP, the drag on the U.S. standard of living was less than 1/10 of one percent per year during the 1970s, less than 1/50 of one percent per year after 1980.

In practice, then, the trend in U.S. living standards is determined by our own rate of productivity growth—full stop. International competition has nothing to do with it.

If that's the case, however, what does it mean when people talk about U.S. "competitiveness"?

The answer, sadly, is that it almost always means that they don't know what they are talking about.

living standards that Japan has experienced since 1950—depends almost entirely on productivity growth.

Nor are living standards the only thing for which national productivity growth is the decisive factor. Shifts in national power are, in the end, dominated by productivity. Since World War II, productivity growth in Britain has averaged about 1.5 percent a year; in Japan it has averaged 7 percent. Britain won the war, and Japan lost; yet Britain has become a third-rank power, while Japan is on the verge of becoming a first-rank one.

In this light the slowdown of American productivity growth since the early 1970s becomes the most important single fact about our economy. Over the first 70 years of this century, American output per worker rose at an average annual rate of 2.3 percent. During the 1950s and 1960s that rate was 2.8 percent. Since 1970, however, our economy has delivered average annual productivity growth of only about 1 percent. Had productivity over the last 25 years grown as fast as it did for the first 70 years of this century, our living standards would now be at least 25 percent higher than they are.

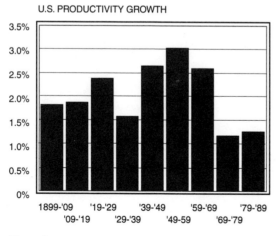

Figure 6
The two decades since 1970 saw the worst U.S. productivity performance of the century.

Compared with the problem of slow productivity growth, all our other long-term economic concerns—foreign competition, the industrial base, lagging technology, deteriorating infrastructure, and so on—are minor issues. Or more accurately, they matter only to the extent that they may have an impact on our productivity growth.

Obviously, then, productivity must be a key political issue, right? Wrong. Economists and business managers occasionally attempt to make it an issue, but their efforts are largely ignored. Nor is this simply a matter of public ignorance. Even among the experts, be they think-tank intellectuals or academic economists, stagnant American productivity is not a fashionable topic. Of course it's important, agrees anyone who thinks about it; but there's nothing much to do about it, so why make a fuss?

This apathy among the experts becomes a little more comprehensible if we ask how economists answer two central questions about America's productivity slump: Why did it happen? And what can we do about it? The answer to both is the same: We don't know.

Start with the first question: Why did productivity growth, which did so well in the 1950s and 1960s, slow to a crawl thereafter?

When the productivity slowdown was still a new event, many people thought that it could be attributed to the energy crisis. The timing was right: The productivity slowdown first became apparent in the five years following the worldwide oil crisis of 1973. This theory was reinforced by the fact that productivity slowed everywhere, not just in the United States. Indeed, the slowdown in West Germany and Japan was even greater than in America (although growth was faster in both countries both before and after the slowdown).

Many economists were never happy with the energy crisis explanation of the productivity slowdown, for a variety of technical reasons. But that technical debate has now become moot: In the 1980s energy prices fell sharply—in real terms almost back to their 1973 levels. If the energy crisis of the 1970s caused the productivity slump, then the reverse energy crisis of the 1980s should have spurred a corresponding productivity boom. It didn't.

This left economists with a set of explanations for the productivity slump that are little more than sophisticated cocktail party chatter. Conservative economists predictably place the blame on increased government regulation—yet productivity growth has been higher in the highly regulated economies of Western Europe than in the United States, and America's move to deregulation in the 1980s has not borne fruit in any reacceleration of growth.

Other economists point to the long-term effects of the social upheavals of the 1960s on mores, motivation, and the quality of education—what might be called "the baby boomer theory"—though this is not what you call serious economic analysis. As MIT economist Robert Solow has put it, most discussions of poor productivity performance end in "a blaze of amateur sociology."

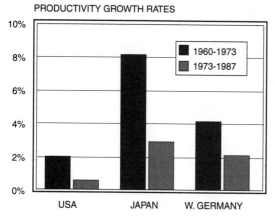

Figure 7
Productivity growth slowed around the world in the early 1970s.

So we really don't know why productivity growth ground to a near halt. That makes it hard to answer the other question: What can we do to speed it up?

There is a standard economist's answer. Unfortunately, it is fairly depressing. If you want more output, say the economists, provide more inputs. Give your workers more capital to work with, and better education, and they will be more productive. And how are we to do these things? Simple: Suffer. Consume less now, so that more resources are available for investment. Send your children to school for more hours, and pay for the extra teachers and classrooms this requires. Do these things, and though you may be worse off right now, eventually they will pay off and living standards will rise. Ten years from now—or is it 20?—our productivity will be sufficiently higher to make up for present sacrifices.

This is not an answer that inspires fervent political support—especially when one bears in mind that the causes of the productivity slump are not obviously tied to declining investment in plant and equipment or in education. In fact, the American economy placed about as high a share of its resources into investment, and a higher share into education, in the 1970s and 1980s as it did in the 1950s and 1960s. It just didn't work as well. So the orthodox prescription for accelerating productivity growth calls on us to make unprecedented efforts, which will depress our living standards in the short run, to offset an undiagnosed ailment. This is the kind of grim advice that has caused economics to be called "the dismal science."

Can't economists think of anything more cheerful to propose? In the late 1970s, when the productivity slowdown was still news, the question of how to get growth going again called forth enthusiastic advocates of a variety of schemes. The most popular nostrums generally separated along left-right lines. On the left, there were the advocates of "industrial policy": people like Robert Reich and Lester Thurow, who thought that by playing a more active role in the marketplace, the government could accelerate productivity growth. On the right, there were supply-siders: people like Arthur Laffer and Jude Wanniski, who believed that getting the government *out* of the marketplace would unleash a wave of private sector dynamism. Although these groups were at opposite ends of the political spectrum, they had much in common. They were outside the academic mainstream, being either economic heretics like Thurow or Laffer, or noneconomists like Reich (a lawyer) or Wanniski (a journalist). And they offered the political system alternatives to the dreary virtue preached by the economics establishment. They offered free lunches—a chance to invigorate the economy without pain.

When Ronald Reagan was elected, the supply-siders got a chance to try out their ideas. Unfortunately, they failed. It was not an abject failure that left the economy in ruins—the American economy clearly did well enough in the 1980s to satisfy most voters. While there are some economists who think that the policies of the Reagan years stored up disaster for America's future, such predictions of doom carry little political weight. But what supply-side economics in power actually delivered was so far short of what it promised that all the fire went out of the movement. The Republicans won the 1988 election, but the supply-siders were not part of the victory party. Bush's economic team consisted of what the English call "Tory wets": Although they were nominally free-market conservatives, they were unwilling to contemplate further radical surgery on the economy, and they even were tempted to re-regulate in such areas as the environment and financial markets.

The apostles of industrial policy got their own, more limited chance at power under Bill Clinton. Robert Reich became secretary of labor; the president is known to be an admirer of Lester Thurow's books. But the one-time advocates of a comprehensive industrial policy have toned down their proposals to a far smaller

scale. In early 1993 the new administration introduced with some
fanfare a set of subsidies and technological initiatives that might
be called an industrial policy, but the sum involved was only $4
billion per year—pocket change in a $6 trillion economy. The
political system simply has no appetite for a really major experiment in industrial policy.

So what are we going to do about productivity growth in the
United States? Nothing.

Well, not exactly nothing. There are various things the government can do that might accelerate productivity growth without
great political risks, from encouraging higher educational standards to supporting a few industry research consortia. These
things will be tried, and some of them may even work a little. But
the basic political consensus at present is that a low rate of productivity growth is something America can live with. We can
hope that something will turn up, and that productivity growth
will accelerate of its own accord. As we'll see in chapter 15, there
are even signs that our wish may be granted. But we won't do
much more than wish.

This, then, is our first big issue. Productivity growth is the single most important factor affecting our economic well-being. But it
is not a policy issue, because we are not going to do anything
about it.

For the typical American family, the past 20 years have been characterized by a remarkable lack of either progress or decline: median family income, at least as measured by the standard statistics, was about the same in 1995 as it was in 1973. But matters have been very different for the atypical families: the rich and the poor. The rich have become a great deal richer, while the poor have become significantly poorer.

It is important to realize not only how dramatic this widening of income inequality has been, but how much of a departure it represents from previous experience. A useful way to make both points is with a picture like Figure 8, which shows the rates of growth of real family income at different "percentiles" of the income distribution. (The family at the 20th percentile has an income that is higher than 20 percent of the population, but lower than the other 80 percent; the family at the 40th percentile has an income higher than 40 percent, but lower than 60 percent, and so on.) The figure, based on Census data, shows growth rates over two periods: the "good years" (the postwar generation from 1947–73) and the subsequent troubled period from 1973 to 1994 (the last year available at time of writing).

The numbers for the postwar generation look like a "picket fence," a row of bars all of nearly the same height. This fence reveals an economy that was not only prospering, but spreading its prosperity widely. Incomes throughout the distribution were rising about 2.5 percent per year—which means that people in virtually all walks of life saw their incomes roughly double over the period. But the bars for the subsequent period look very different: not a picket fence but a staircase, with some of the steps below ground level. They reveal an economy that not only delivered a much slower overall pace of growth, but distributed that disappointing growth very unevenly, with incomes rising steadily among the well-off but stagnating or even declining at the bottom of the scale.

Even these numbers fail to capture the full extent of what happened, because they miss the real extremes. There is pretty good evidence that the incomes of the top 1 percent of families more than doubled over this period. This means that while average family income grew far more slowly after 1973 than before, income growth among the very well-off actually accelerated. And the very top of the income distribution did even better— for example, the compensation of the chief executives of large

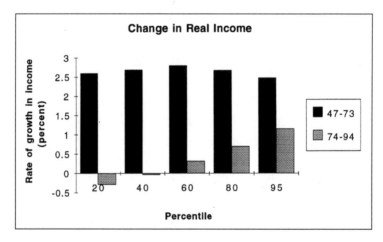

Figure 8
In the 1980s, the poor got poorer while the rich got richer.

corporations more than quadrupled in real terms. Meanwhile, the amount of sheer misery in America surely increased much faster than the official poverty rate, as homelessness and drug addiction spread.

Long-term comparisons of income distribution are fraught with difficulties, but for what it is worth, standard calculations show that the surge in inequality in the United States after 1973 completely reversed the movement toward equality— what economic historian Claudia Goldin has called the Great Compression—that had taken place during the 1930s and 1940s. By the mid-1990s, America was probably about as unequal a society as it had been in the Great Gatsby era of the 1920s.

While some conservatives do not consider income distribution a valid issue for public concern, the changes in that distribution after the mid-1970s had a far more important effect on people's lives than any deliberate government action. After all, even a disastrous policy blunder is unlikely to lower the real incomes of 50 million Americans by 10 percent; yet that is what happened to the poorest fifth of the population after 1973. Not everyone agrees that soaring inequality is a bad thing, but it is a simple fact that the growth of both affluence and poverty in recent decades largely reflected changes in the distribution of income, rather than in its overall level.

There are at least two reasons for arguing that increased inequality changes *overall* welfare for the worse. First, most Americans do care at least a little bit about how well-off others are, and it is hard to argue with the conclusion that an extra thousand dollars of income matters more to a poor family than to someone whose income is already in six digits. Second, the income distribution colors the whole tone of society: A society with few extremes of wealth or poverty is a different, and surely more attractive, place than one with a yawning gulf between rich and poor.

In the long run, income distribution is not as important a determinant of economic well-being as productivity growth, but for the past generation increasing inequality in income distribution, rather than growth in productivity, has been the main source of rising living standards for the top 10 percent of Americans. And the 1980s was the first decade since the 1930s in which large numbers of Americans actually suffered a serious decline in living standards.

Yet income distribution, like productivity growth, is not a policy issue that is on the table. This is partly because we don't fully understand why inequality soared, but mostly because any attempt to reverse its trend appears politically out of bounds.

One reason that action to limit growing income inequality in the United States is difficult is that the growth in inequality is not a simple picture. Old-line leftists, if there are any left, would like to make it a single story—the rich becoming richer by exploiting the poor. But that's just not a reasonable picture of America in the 1990s. For one thing, most of our very poor don't work, which makes it hard to exploit them. For another, the poor had so little to start with that the dollar value of the gains of the rich dwarfs that of the losses of the poor. (In constant dollars, the increase in per family income among the top tenth of the population in the 1980s was about a dozen times as large as the decline among the bottom tenth.)

To tell the story of what happened to income distribution, it is necessary to paint a more complicated picture. At least three separate trends have combined to make our society radically less equal. To begin with, at the very bottom of the scale, the so-called "underclass" grew both more numerous and more miserable. Entirely unrelated, as far as anyone can tell, was a huge increase in the incomes of the very rich. In between, among those who work for a living, the earnings of the relatively unskilled fell while the earnings of the highly skilled rose.

Let's start with the underclass. While there is no generally accepted statistical definition of the underclass, we all know what it means: that largely nonwhite hard core of people caught in a vicious circle of poverty and social collapse. Attempts to measure the size of the underclass, like those of Isabel Sawhill at the Urban Institute, suggest that it began growing during the 1960s, and has continued to grow, perhaps at an accelerating rate, since then. In the 1960s and the 1970s, social programs were expected to cure persistent poverty; in the 1980s, they were widely accused of indirectly perpetuating it. At this point it appears that if you increase spending on the poor, they have more money; if you reduce it, they have less; otherwise, it doesn't make much differ-ence. That is, neither generosity nor niggardliness seems to make much difference to the spread of the underclass. Conservatives argue that the welfare system has reduced incentives and con-tributed to the growth of the underclass; liberals respond that Reagan's cuts in social spending contributed to the growth of the underclass by making it more difficult for the poor to climb out of poverty. Both could be right. The most important causes of the growth in the underclass, however, like the sources of the pro-ductivity slowdown, lie more in the domain of sociology than of economics.

The increased incomes of the rich and very well-off present less of a puzzle than the growth of the underclass. While high incomes have been made in a variety of ways, one source stands out above all: finance. The 1980s were a golden age for financial wheeling and dealing, and the explosion of profits in financial operations has helped swell the ranks of the really rich—those earning hundreds of thousands or even millions a year.

Most Americans live between the stratosphere and the lower depths, and for them the growth in inequality has been yet a dif-ferent story. First, there was the yuppie phenomenon: The rise of two-income professional couples has increased the number of families with $50,000 or more in annual income. Second, wage differentials among occupations widened: the real wages of blue-collar workers have declined fairly steadily for the past 15 years, and earnings of highly educated workers have risen rapidly. (The ratio of earnings of college graduates to those of high school graduates declined during the 1970s from 1.5 to 1.3, then rose to 1.8 during the 1980s.)

What we really don't know is why these phenomena have all happened now. The rise of two-income professional couples reflects the lagged effects of the women's movement, plus the aging of the baby boom generation. The surges in pay differentials and in market manipulation are more mysterious. Politics may have had something to do with it. The Reagan years provided a tolerant climate both for tough bargaining with workers and for financial wheeling and dealing. Other forces, like the decline of smokestack America and the consequent restructuring of the U.S. economy, may also have played a role.

Whatever the reasons for soaring inequality, what can policy do about it? In particular, can anything be done about the extremes of wealth and poverty that have emerged in the past decade?

The problem with poverty, as an issue, is that it has exhausted the patience of the general public. America launched its War on Poverty in the 1960s—a time of rising incomes and widespread optimism about government activism. This "war" was supposed to be social engineering, not merely charity. It was intended not simply to raise the living standards of the poor, but to help them work their way out of poverty. Yet poverty did not decline. Despite sharp increases in aid to the poor between the late 1960s and the mid-1970s, poverty remained as intractable as ever, and the underclass that is the most visible sign of poverty grew alarmingly. Today, relatively few people believe, as so many did in the 1960s, that government can do much to help the poor become more productive; all that it seems able to do is raise their standard of living by giving them more money (and influential books, like Charles Murray's *Losing Ground,* deny even that).

But if aid to the poor is simply charity, then its political base is nothing more than public generosity. In a time of budget deficits and largely static living standards for the average American, such generosity does not come easily. Congress has been willing to throw a few crumbs in the direction of the working poor: a subsidy to their wages through a sort of negative income tax called the Earned Income Tax Credit, and a rise in the minimum wage. But there is no sympathy left for the poor who do not work. The program known as Aid to Families with Dependent Children—which is what most people think of when they speak of "welfare"—was radically scaled back in 1996.

As for the rich, a few public policy initiatives might cut down on some of their sources of income. For example, tighter regulation of financial markets might limit the number of people with incomes in the tens of millions, and a cooled-off financial market might indirectly put some limits on executive pay. For the most part, however, the only way to make the rich less so is to tax them. And indeed, in 1993 the Clinton administration passed tax increases that fell for the most part on families with incomes over $100,000 per year. These tax increases rolled back part—but only part—of the tax cuts these high incomes received from Ronald Reagan. As we've already seen, however, the bulk of the increase in inequality during the 1980s was a growth in the spread of pre-tax, not post-tax income. So undoing some of Reagan's generosity to the rich made only a small dent in the trend.

So income distribution, like productivity growth, is a policy issue with little prospect for serious policy action. The growing gap between rich and poor is arguably the central fact about economic life in America. But no policy changes now under discussion seem likely to do much to narrow this gap.

3   Employment and Unemployment

In the middle of 1996 only 5.3 percent of the work force was unemployed. This was a slightly lower rate of unemployment than in 1978 (6.0 percent), and somewhat higher than in 1970 (4.8 percent). That may not sound impressive, but in fact it was a remarkable achievement. During the 1970s and 1980s huge numbers of workers entered the U.S. labor force—baby boomers, women, immigrants. The American economy found jobs for almost all of them.

America's success in creating jobs stands out especially well when contrasted with the experience of other countries. In Europe, in particular, virtually no new jobs have been created since the early 1970s. So even though Europe's labor force grew much more slowly than America's, unemployment increased fivefold.

Why does unemployment matter? Partly because high unemployment means that potentially productive workers are not being used, preventing the economy from producing as much as it might; partly because high unemployment breeds persistent poverty. Beyond this, however, the availability of jobs plays a key role in the way our society hangs together. A society in which young people can routinely expect to get jobs on leaving school, and to remain gainfully employed except for occasional spells for their adult lives, is going to be a very different place from one in which work is a privilege that is unavailable to many people—even if the welfare state is generous to the unemployed, as it is in much of Europe. It is a value judgment to say that a working society, other things equal, is a better society, but it is a value judgment that most Americans would share.

If unemployment is such a bad thing, then, why does the United States content itself with 5 percent or more instead of trying for something lower—say, 3 percent, which would add more than two million additional jobs? The answer is not what you might think. It is not that there is insufficient demand for the services of unemployed workers. Creating demand for workers is not usually a problem for the U.S. economy: The Federal Reserve Board can create as much demand as it likes with a phone call. The problem is how to do that without also creating inflation. The principal constraint on reducing unemployment is the fear of the Federal Reserve that too low an unemployment rate will lead to accelerating inflation.

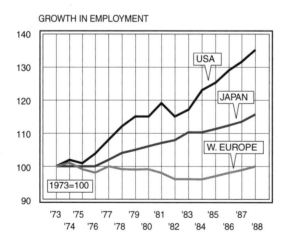

Figure 9
U.S. employment has grown rapidly since the early 1970s; this is in sharp contrast to the experience elsewhere, especially in Europe.

Since the late 1960s, when Milton Friedman and a number of other economists proposed the concept, most economists have agreed that at any given time there is a certain level of unemployment that is consistent with stable inflation. If the government tries to increase demand to drive unemployment below that rate, it will pay the price of accelerating inflation. If the government wants to reduce the inflation rate, it must reduce demand so as to drive unemployment above this rate. The critical rate of unemployment was dubbed by Friedman the "natural rate"; other economists, disliking the suggestion that there was something good about joblessness, have proposed the alternative "nonaccelerating inflation rate of unemployment," or NAIRU.

The logic behind the idea of a NAIRU may be seen by considering the example of an economy where the government is trying to provide very full employment by keeping demand high.

Suppose that when the government starts its program of stimulus, the economy has a history of more or less stable prices. Once demand is increased, however, so that most factories run at capacity and nearly everyone can get a job, there will be a strong tendency for prices to rise. In such an economy firms will feel free to raise prices, and workers will demand wage increases over and above their rate of productivity growth. So in attempting to lower the unemployment rate from, say, 6 to 3 percent, the government might find that its formerly stable prices give way to an inflation rate of, say, 5 percent.

Now maybe the government is willing to make this trade-off. Perhaps it regards 6 percent unemployment as a much more serious problem than 5 percent inflation. Unfortunately, what it will soon find is that the trade-off is not stable. The reason is that persistent inflation gets built into people's expectations. After a few years of 5 percent inflation, workers will come to expect this inflation to continue and will make demands for wage increases over and above it. Firms will set prices higher based on the expectation

that their costs and the prices of their competitors will rise at a 5
percent rate until their next price revision. And the government
will find that to keep unemployment at 3 percent, it needs to
accept not 5 percent inflation, but 10 percent.

If the government still thinks the trade-off is worthwhile, then
after a few more years it will find the necessary rate of inflation to
be 15 percent—and so on. In the end, the only way to keep unemployment very low will be to accept an ever-accelerating inflation
rate. And while 5 percent or even 10 percent inflation may be
acceptable, 100 percent or 1,000,000 percent are not.

So to avoid ever-accelerating inflation, the government must
accept an unemployment rate that is sufficiently high that workers
do not on average demand real wage increases that exceed their
productivity growth, and firms do not try to raise their prices
faster than their costs. The minimum unemployment rate that
will restrain inflation is the NAIRU.

The NAIRU is not an immutable, unchanging feature of the
economy. Changes in long-term government policies and in the
economy's structure can raise or lower it. For example, restrictive
government policies that make it costly for firms to add employees can raise the NAIRU. Many economists blame such policies
for "Eurosclerosis"—the persistent rise in European unemployment rates after 1970. Demographic changes may also matter:
Young workers characteristically have high unemployment rates,
so an aging of the work force may lower the NAIRU. The important point, however, is that whatever the NAIRU happens to be at
any given time, it places an obstacle to any attempt to expand
employment by increasing demand.

Most estimates of the NAIRU for the United States currently
place it somewhere between 5 and 6 percent. Figure 10 shows an
illustration of how these estimates are made. On the vertical axis
is the *change* in the rate of increase in consumer prices—for
instance, if inflation goes from 3 percent to 5 percent, we indicate

this as a value of +2. On the horizontal axis is the rate of unemployment. The scatter of points represents America's experience between 1973 and 1995, with each point representing a particular year. The relationship is not a particularly neat one—this is economics, not physics—but on the whole we see that inflation tended to rise when the unemployment rate was low, to fall when it was high. Notice in particular the points corresponding to the early 1980s, when very high unemployment helped bring a significant reduction in the inflation rate; these points will play a key role in the story when we examine inflation later.

A line plotted through these points crosses zero at about 6.6 percent unemployment; thus, based on the historical record, we would expect that an unemployment rate of less than 6 percent would be associated with accelerating inflation. In fact the unemployment rate in 1996 was closer to 5 percent than to 6 percent, with at best a slight increase in inflation. This may reflect a downward shift in the NAIRU—as baby boomers have become older and women more experienced, the amount of "frictional"

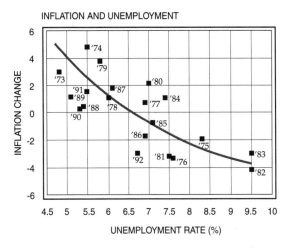

Figure 10
Inflation tends to rise when the unemployment rate is low, to fall when the unemployment rate is high.

unemployment may have declined—or it may just represent luck in what is after all an imprecise relationship.

The important point is that for the United States the NAIRU seems to have been fairly stable, or even falling, for the past 20 years. This means that there was no long-term tendency for the unemployment rate to increase—and that is quite a tribute to the adaptive ability of the American economy. As we have seen, unemployment rates in Europe have risen inexorably over time. The U.S. economy might easily have had big problems creating enough jobs for the enormous number of women and baby boomers who entered its labor force over the past decade. With productivity growth so sluggish, and real earnings per worker stagnant or declining, one might have expected worker frustration to lead to large wage demands. As it turned out, America's highly competitive and flexible labor markets made room for all the new entrants and limited wage increases to rates consistent with our slow productivity growth.

Of course 5-6 percent unemployment is not zero. Shouldn't there be a program to reduce the NAIRU, so that we could have 4 percent or less unemployment? Well, maybe—but there is no widespread agreement among economists about what kinds of policies, if any, would accomplish that goal. Politicians may make a few symbolic efforts, say by offering training to the long-term unemployed, but we can be sure that if the Clinton administration is able to keep unemployment near 5 percent, it will be well satisfied.

II

Chronic Aches and Pains

If you want to ask what really matters for the economic welfare of large numbers of Americans, productivity, income distribution, and employment are probably 90 percent of the story. If you ask what motivates actual legislation and administration initiatives, however, these issues are probably less than 5 percent of the agenda. The reason is not that policymakers don't appreciate the importance of these central issues; it is that they see little within the normal range of policy that they can do about them. Any serious effort to increase productivity growth, or to reverse the sharp increase in income inequality, or to restructure our labor markets to get closer to true full employment, would take a degree of boldness that is rare in economic policy. Attempts to change the economic system in a fundamental way, like Franklin Roosevelt's (or Ronald Reagan's), occur only in the face of economic crisis. And while there are good reasons not to be completely happy about America's economy in the mid-1990s, it isn't in crisis—so the big issues don't move actual policy.

But the fact that the most important economic issues are, in effect, out of range does not mean that economic policymaking comes to a halt. It just means that debate focuses on issues that, while less important than, say, productivity growth, are closer to the level that might be a subject of real policy. The issues discussed in the next two chapters, while still not the direct object of legislation, are nevertheless close enough to the ground that current policy discussions are directly affected by the desire to do something about them.

There isn't as much inevitability in the choice of policy problems to discuss as there is in the case of the big issues. Twenty years ago, energy policy would surely have made the list; today it has faded as a major concern. A decade from now, environmental economics may well be on the list. Right now, however, the two most obvious policy problems to discuss are the trade deficit and inflation.

4   The Trade Deficit

One day recently I had a meeting in New York. Before leaving, I set my Sharp VCR to record a television program I would miss while away. Then I drove my Volvo to the airport, boarded an Airbus A310, and while in transit finished some notes for the meeting on my Toshiba laptop computer. My suit was made in Hong Kong, my coffee cup in Portugal. It is quite possible that my breakfast cereal was the only American-made product I encountered all morning.

This was not a surprising experience in the 1990s, but it would have been very unusual just 20 years ago. It is sometimes hard to remember that as recently as 1981, the United States exported as large a value of manufactured goods as it imported, and it remained the world's clear leader in high technology. Until the late 1970s, U.S. aircraft and computer manufacturers had no major rivals abroad; imports of foreign automobiles and consumer goods were largely restricted to the low end of the market.

The massive trade deficits that now seem a permanent feature of the U.S. scene emerged quite quickly between 1981 and 1984. In 1981 the U.S. trade picture still looked healthy. Exports of manufactured goods more than paid for manufactured imports, while exports of agricultural goods and earnings from overseas assets more than covered the cost of oil imports. The broadest measure

of U.S. trade, the so-called current account of the balance of payments, was in modest surplus, as it had been for most of the century. By mid-1984, however, the current account was in deficit at
an annual rate of more than $100 billion, and despite some
improvements in the late 1980s, there is little prospect that it will
move into balance for years to come. (In fact, it is more likely to
increase.)

Many critics of American economic policy point to the trade
deficit as evidence that our prosperity is built on sand. The general public, while sanguine about the economy generally, is worried about the trade deficit; rising public concern led to the
passage of the 1988 Trade Act, a law that, while not overtly protectionist, certainly carried a tougher tone than its predecessors.
Yet there are also respectable voices claiming that the deficit pre-
sents no problem, or even that it is a sign of American strength.
Before we even ask why the United States has begun to run a
trade deficit, we need to ask why the trade deficit matters.

Why worry about the trade deficit?

Ask the man in the street why a trade deficit is a bad thing, and he
will probably answer that it costs America jobs. The point seems
obvious enough: If we spend more on imports than foreigners
spend on our exports, the result is reduced demand for American
labor. The immediate job costs of international competition are
easy to understand: plants closed because of competition from
imports, workers laid off because of the drying up of export markets. At first glance the numbers can seem very impressive.
Consider, for example, the situation in 1990. In that year the
United States ran a current account deficit of $98 billion, about
1.8 percent of national income. If we could somehow have kept
those dollars at home, the extra demand would have been
enough to employ about two million more workers. It is natural to

imagine that those two million "lost jobs" are the crux of the problem.

Yet focusing on the employment effects of the trade deficit is not only misleading—it is slightly more than 100 percent wrong. America's trade deficit problem has nothing to do with jobs. As we have seen, the 1980s were actually a time of quite satisfactory job creation. New jobs created in sectors that are insulated from international competition, such as services, far outpaced any job losses in export or import-competing sectors. Not only did the United States do very well at creating jobs in the 1980s despite the ballooning trade deficit, it would have done little if any better—indeed, probably a bit worse—had the trade deficit somehow been prevented.

The reason is that the amount of employment offered in the U.S. economy is normally limited by supply, not demand. It's not very hard to increase demand: The problem is that increasing demand too much leads to inflationary pressures. Driving the unemployment rate below 5 to 6 percent will lead to accelerating inflation. In 1990, U.S. unemployment was, if anything, at the low

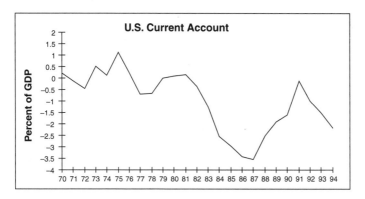

Figure 11
The U.S. economy generally ran small surpluses on its current account, the broadest measure of its international trade, until 1981. In the 1980s, however, the nation plunged into a deep trade deficit. This deficit peaked in 1987 and has declined since then, especially when measured as a share of national income.

end of the safe range, so we could not have had fuller employment without higher inflation.

Imagine that in 1990 America could somehow have eliminated its trade deficit at a single stroke—say, by imposing quotas on imports. This would have added to the current demand for labor the demand for another two million workers to fill the jobs currently "lost" because of the deficit. But would employment really have risen by two million? Of course not. First of all, the United States does not have two million suitable workers available (or the plant capacity to employ them). America in 1990 was not like America in 1938, with a huge reserve army of easily employable workers ready to go to work given sufficient demand. Most of the five million or so unemployed were either unskilled or part of the inevitable "frictional" unemployment that occurs as workers change jobs or outmoded plants close. The main effect of an increase in demand would have been not to increase employment but to bid up wages. To put it another way, adding two million jobs, if we could have done it, would have driven the U.S. unemployment rate down to around 3 percent. But that isn't possible, or at any rate not for very long: At that low an unemployment rate, inflation would begin to accelerate rapidly.

In reality, of course, that wouldn't happen. The Federal Reserve Board would raise interest rates to choke off demand and cool down the economy. Since the economy already had more or less as many workers employed as it could manage without inflationary pressure, this offset would destroy roughly as many jobs as eliminating the trade deficit would create. They wouldn't be the same jobs: Construction and service workers would be laid off while manufacturing workers were called back. But overall employment would not rise.

Attempts to reduce the trade deficit might even have led indirectly to a *fall* in employment, at least for a while, as the government either drove down the exchange value of the dollar or restricted imports, both of which are inflationary in their own right. To keep inflation under control would therefore have taken a little extra tightening on the domestic side. So we would probably have had slightly fewer jobs without the trade deficit than we do with it.

Alert readers will have noticed that this argument was carefully applied to 1990—a year in which the U.S. economy was at or below the NAIRU. But what about when the economy is in a recession, as it was in 1992? Didn't the trade deficit cost jobs then?

The answer here is a little more complicated. Other things equal, the United States would have had lower unemployment in 1992 if it had had a smaller trade deficit. This was because the U.S. economy as a whole was suffering a shortfall in demand, and reducing the trade deficit is one way to increase demand. But there are lots of other ways to increase demand, such as cutting

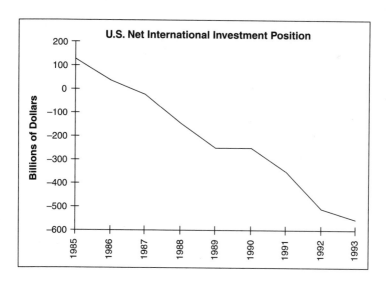

Figure 12
The trade deficits of the 1980s changed the United States from the world's largest creditor to its largest debtor, reversing the results of 60 years of investment abroad in only four years.

interest rates, reducing taxes, or increasing public spending; all of these are pleasant things to do in their own right. The constraint on doing enjoyable things to increase demand is the risk that we will overdo it and create inflation problems—and a smaller trade deficit would increase that risk.

The point is that although the U.S. economy does sometimes stumble into recessions, our ability to keep unemployment down is ultimately limited by supply, not demand. A lower trade deficit might seem to mean more jobs in a particular year, but over the long run the trade deficit and the average rate of unemployment are pretty much unrelated.

If the trade deficit doesn't cost jobs, why worry about it? One answer is that we shouldn't. Herbert Stein, Chairman of the President's Council of Economic Advisers under Richard Nixon, has flatly declared the trade deficit to be a "nonproblem." A significant minority of economists agrees with him. Some even believe that it represents a sign of America's strength. But even these optimists would concede that the trade deficit does have a cost: a gradual mortgaging of future U.S. income to foreigners.

After all, the United States does not get its imports for free. When we buy more goods and services from foreigners than we sell to them, we must give the foreigners something else to cover the difference. What we give them is assets: The U.S. trade deficit in the 1980s was financed by a steady sale of American assets—stocks, bonds, real estate, and, increasingly, whole corporations to foreigners.

The U.S. Department of Commerce regularly reports an estimate of what it calls the U.S. net international investment position: the difference between the value of American assets abroad and foreign assets in the United States. That position has been in the black since World War I, when Britain liquidated many of its holdings here and borrowed heavily from U.S. banks to finance its war effort. The U.S. net investment position grew substantially in the 1950s and 1960s as U.S. corporations went multinational. Even during the 1970s the United States continued to invest more abroad than foreigners did here.

But that investment position quickly evaporated. At the end of 1983 our claims on foreigners were still worth $268 billion more than foreign claims on the United States by the end of 1991 the situation was more than reversed, with foreign assets here exceeding our assets abroad by $382 billion.

What's wrong with being a net debtor? There is one definite cost. There are also some vaguer risks.

The definite cost is, by definition, that you owe people money. From now on, the United States will be obliged to deliver a stream of interest payments to foreign bondholders, rents to foreign landowners, and dividends to foreign stockholders. The numbers are fairly staggering. In 1981 U.S. net investment income from abroad was $34 billion; in 1989 it was negative; and the number will continue to worsen as foreigners expand their U.S. holdings. Our payments to foreigners are a direct drain on our resources, and the longer the trade deficits continue, the larger this drain will become.

But America is a huge country; it can shrug off burdens that would crush smaller nations. The spectacular decline in our net investment income since 1981, measured as a share of GNP, amounts to about a 1.5 percent drain on our economy—not a trivial number, but hardly ruinous. If the United States were to continue to sell assets at current rates, the burden of paying foreign investors could rise by an additional 2 to 3 percent of GNP by the end of the century. Again, this is serious, but no cause for panic. The United States could continue to run trade deficits as big as that of 1989 for a long time before the payment burden becomes unsupportable.

But what about the risks? The big economic risk is that as the United States becomes a massive net debtor it will be exposed to financial crises whenever the confidence of foreign investors is shaken. This is what happened to most of Latin America at the beginning of the 1980s. Banks lent the Latin nations large sums for a decade, then abruptly cut off the flow when their confidence began to waver, precipitating an economic crisis. The vision of the United States as a giant Argentina may be unlikely, but no one should dismiss it out of hand.

The other risks are political. First, there is at least some case to be made that growing foreign ownership of U.S. assets compromises our national sovereignty. We tended to dismiss this argument as patently silly when we were the foreign investors who wanted to invest in other countries. Now that the shoe is on the other foot, it seems more compelling. Second, both the trade deficit and the growing foreign stake here tend to feed crude forms of economic nationalism at home, increasing the risks of a trade war. In fact, it was primarily concern over growing protectionist pressure that led the Reagan administration to start talking down the dollar in 1985.

The measurable costs of the trade deficit, then, are serious but not devastating. The risks are uncertain but worrisome. There isn't any reason to panic about the trade deficit, but getting it down would make everyone breathe a little easier.

But before we start talking about bringing the trade deficit down, we need to ask why we have a deficit in the first place.

Why the trade deficit?

In 1982 Martin Feldstein, the Harvard professor newly appointed Chairman of the President's Council of Economic Advisers, found a new reason to condemn the emerging budget deficit. At a time when most critics of that deficit worried that it would lead to inflation, or perhaps to high interest rates, Feldstein argued that it would lead to something quite different: unprecedented *trade* deficits. Initially his audiences were bemused. Over time, however, as the budget and trade deficits mounted together, the idea of "twin deficits" became a cliché—as well as a target for bitter attack.

Feldstein was, of course, deliberately oversimplifying. His emphasis on the linkage between the two deficits had two purposes: first, to persuade his "what-me-worry" political masters that they should do something about the budget deficit; and second, to answer protectionists who blamed the U.S. trade deficit on unfair foreign trade practices. Today, few economists believe in a simple one-to-one linkage between the budget and trade deficits. Yet a revised version of the "twin deficit" story is still the best explanation for the emergence of unprecedented trade deficits in the 1980s.

The basic story runs as follows: Beginning in 1981, U.S. national saving began to fall sharply. Only part of that fall was a result of the budget deficit—hence the need to qualify the "twin deficit" view a bit—while part of it represented a change in the behavior of households. In any case, what happened was that U.S. national saving began falling well short of U.S. investment demand, which remained strong. If the U.S. economy had not had access to world capital markets, this saving shortfall would have produced a crunch that pushed interest rates sky-high. Instead, the United States was able to turn to foreigners to fill the gap. Much of U.S. investment was financed, not out of our own savings, but through the sale of assets to foreigners.

As a matter of straightforward accounting, the United States always buys exactly as much as it sells from the rest of the world. If it sells foreigners more assets than it buys, it must correspondingly buy more goods than it sells. So the emergent U.S. dependence on foreign capital to finance its investment had as an inevitable counterpart the emergence of a trade deficit. The ultimate cause of the trade deficit therefore lies in a decline in U.S. saving—partly, but not entirely, due to the budget deficit.

Although this mainstream story is now widely accepted, many readers may feel that it is missing something. Where are all the real things that affect international trade? What happened to the dollar? What happened to U.S. competitiveness? Don't these have something to do with the trade deficit, too?

The answer is that they do, and then again at a deeper level they don't. That is, at any point in time, when we discuss the U.S. trade deficit, the level of the dollar and the international competitiveness of U.S. industry clearly matter. The ups and downs of the dollar, in particular, have been spectacular since 1980. When the dollar rose against the currencies of our major competitors in the first half of the 1980s, it sharply raised the prices of U.S. goods relative to foreign, playing a key role in encouraging imports and discouraging exports. Some of this effect was reversed when the dollar fell again after 1985. Yet even though exchange rates play a crucial role in international trade, at a deeper level capital flows are the real story.

The relationships among capital flows, exchange rates, and the U.S. trade balance have become the subject of a peculiarly nasty debate in recent years—peculiar, because the subject is relatively technical and straightforward. Yet hardly a week goes by without an angry debate between mainstream economists, who assign great importance to the exchange rate, and their critics.

One line of criticism comes from the right. Many conservatives believe that the world should return to a gold standard—that the value of each currency should be fixed in terms of gold. Since this would also fix the values of currencies in terms of each other, these conservatives are uncomfortable with the idea that changes in exchange rates may sometimes play a useful role. So they welcome the arguments of academics like Stanford's Ronald McKinnon, who declares that exchange rates are irrelevant to trade.

Why devaluation is sometimes a good idea

At a basic level, the United States has a trade deficit because it spends more than it earns, and Japan has a trade surplus because it earns more than it spends. That's why any attempt to solve trade imbalances simply by shifting demand from foreign to U.S. goods will fail. But if this is the case, why bother with expenditure-switching policies at all? Why is devaluing the dollar sometimes a good idea?

The reason is that trying to solve the U.S. trade deficit just by cutting U.S. spending and raising demand abroad will not lead to the right *kind* of demand. Despite the rapid increase in international trade over the past 40 years, the world economy is still far form being perfectly integrated. Most of the income of U.S. residents is spent on goods and services produced here; the same is true of Europe and Japan. As a result, most of a reduction in U.S. expenditure will be reflected, other things equal, in a fall in demand for U.S. goods and services; only a small fraction of an increase in expenditure in Europe or Japan will be spent on U.S. products.

To see the problem this causes, consider the example illustrated in the accompanying table. Imagine that the United States reduces its spending by $100 billion, while the rest of the world (ROW) simultaneously increases its demand by the same amount. Does this translate smoothly into a $100 billion reduction in the trade deficit? Unfortunately, it does not. At least $80 billion of the reduction in U.S. spending is likely to represent a fall in demand for goods and services produced here, with only $20 billion representing a fall in demand for imports. Meanwhile, no more than $10 billion of the rise in spending of the rest of the world is likely to be spent on U.S. goods, with $90 billion spent on ROW products. The result is therefore a net reduction in demand for U.S. products of $70 billion, and an equal increase in demand for ROW products. Instead of a smooth reduction in the U.S. trade deficit, we would get a combination of recession in the United States and inflation abroad. To make the adjustment work, some way has to be found to *switch* $70 billion in spending from ROW to U.S. products. The easiest way to do this is to lower the foreign exchange value of the dollar, which makes U.S. goods cheaper to ROW residents and ROW goods more expensive to U.S. residents.

The lesson of this example is that while devaluing the dollar cannot by itself solve a trade deficit, it can be crucial as part of a deficit-reduction strategy.

	Total demand	Demand for U.S. products	Demand for ROW products
United States	−100	−80	−20
ROW	+100	+10	+90
Total	0	−70	+70

Other critics come from the left—people who want an active government role in promoting exports and limiting imports, and who dislike the idea that a market mechanism like the exchange rate can do the job. They therefore like the arguments of pundits such as the *American Prospect*'s Robert Kuttner, who wants us to use a tough trade policy to bring our trade deficit down, and who accuses the advocates of a low dollar of wanting to balance trade by cutting American wages.

As usual, the intellectual debate has been warped by the political imperatives of the moment—a distortion that takes place all the more readily because it takes a little sophistication to understand what the exchange rate does and does not do.

The important thing to grasp is that the exchange rate is a crucial part of the *mechanism* that determines the trade balance, without being an independent *cause* of the trade balance. If this sounds unduly metaphysical, consider the following analogy. Think of the U.S. trade balance as an automobile. The exchange rate is not that car's engine—it is more like the drive shaft, with desired capital flows providing the motive power. In other words, changes in the exchange rate play a crucial role in translating changes in desired capital flows into changes in the trade balance, but the root cause of the trade imbalance lies elsewhere.

America's experience in the first half of the 1980s provides a good example. National saving fell—that is, consumption spending increased as a share of national income. But investment spending remained high, because an inflow of foreign capital took the place of the reduced flow of domestic saving. So overall spending in the U.S. economy rose faster than national income. The only way for an economy to spend more than it earns, however, is to import more than it exports—to run a trade deficit. So it was inevitable that the United States would develop a large trade deficit.

It was not inevitable that this trade deficit would emerge via a strong dollar. The Federal Reserve could have expanded the supply of dollars to keep the exchange rate low. But this would have led to an inflationary boom that sucked in imports (an experience that Britain had in the 1980s). As it turned out, however, the Federal Reserve kept inflation down by raising interest rates, which made dollar-denominated assets attractive to foreigners and so led to a rise of the dollar against other currencies. This rise in the dollar, by making U.S. goods expensive compared with foreign, then led to the emergence of the unprecedented trade deficits that were the counterpart of the capital inflows. The point is that while the rise of the dollar was a central part of the story as it actually played out, it is still correct to say that the U.S. trade deficit was essentially caused by the fall of national saving, which led to massive imports of capital.

What about competitiveness? It is obvious to everyone that the once-vaunted U.S. superiority over other nations in technology and quality has eroded over the past generation. Doesn't this loss of superiority help explain the rise in our trade deficit? The answer is no. If U.S. national saving had remained high, the loss of competitive advantage would not have led to a trade deficit. It would instead have led to a fall in the dollar, which would have compensated for the loss of technology and quality by making U.S. goods relatively cheaper. This is what happened in the 1970s. The United States had about the same trade balance at the end of the 1970s as it did at the beginning, but with a much lower dollar. This isn't to say that a dollar that declines every year is without costs. Competitiveness does matter—but not for the trade deficit.

We'll come back to exchange rates and competitiveness when we look at dollar policy in chapter 9. For now, the important thing to recognize is that the root cause of the emergence of trade deficits in the 1980s was America's low national saving rate, which led it to import large quantities of capital. The next question is: What can be done about it?

Can the trade deficit be eliminated?

Can the United States eliminate its trade deficit? Of course it can. When it really wants to (or really has to), virtually any country can run a trade surplus. Most Latin American countries quickly shifted from large trade deficits to large trade surpluses when the debt crisis struck in the early 1980s. The United States may not want to emulate that experience, but it shows that trade deficits are not immutable facts. If America continues to run a trade deficit, it is because it chooses not to take the steps that would eliminate it.

The solution to a trade deficit has two parts. Expenditure must be both *switched* and *reduced*. Somehow people must be persuaded to switch their demand from foreign to U.S. goods—either by reducing the value of the dollar or by imposing tariffs and import quotas. But this isn't enough. There must also be a policy to reduce the level of domestic demand, so that the expenditure-switching policies don't just feed inflation.

That, of course, is the problem. We can all agree that it would be nice if Americans could sell more to foreigners and buy less, although we may argue about how best to arrange that happy event. Reducing domestic demand is another matter. Expenditure reduction hurts, and there is only one reliable way to do it: balance the federal budget, or even move it into surplus. Unless we do that, there is nothing much we can—or should—do about the trade deficit.

It's important to understand why both switching and reducing are needed to eliminate the trade deficit. Let's therefore imagine the consequences of two alternative strategies for reducing the trade deficit *without* a cut in domestic demand: an aggressive effort to drive the dollar down, making U.S. goods cheaper on world markets; and a protectionist policy that imposes new restrictions on U.S. imports.

There is no question that the government—or more accurately the Federal Reserve—could drive the dollar down if it wanted to. All it has to do is increase the supply of dollars. The resulting fall in the foreign exchange value of the dollar would certainly help U.S. exporters and make it easier for American firms to compete with imports at home.

Unfortunately, there is a side consequence of printing dollars: inflation. Any policy that tries to drive the dollar down other than by reducing our need for foreign capital will necessarily feed inflation. This is an unwanted consequence in and of itself, and it also undermines the initial objective of the policy, because inflation reduces the competitiveness of U.S. producers at any given exchange rate. The eventual result of an effort to drive the dollar down will be to raise U.S. prices by roughly the same proportion as the dollar falls, so that U.S. competitiveness is unaffected. The result, then, would be inflation with no gain on the trade front.

A protectionist policy could certainly reduce U.S. imports. But if U.S. savings have not been increased, lower imports will mean a lower supply of dollars to the foreign exchange market and thus a stronger dollar; the rise in the dollar will cut into exports and encourage increases in whichever imports are not restricted. The dollar will probably rise enough to just about eliminate the favorable impact of the import restrictions on the trade balance. The Federal Reserve could, of course, prevent the dollar from rising by printing more dollars—but this merely brings back the inflation problem.

The moral of both of these scenarios is fairly simple. There isn't much that the United States can do about its trade deficit simply by trying to encourage exports or discourage imports. The only way to cut the trade deficit successfully is to accompany export-promoting and import-cutting measures with domestic policies that reduce domestic demand—in effect making room for a trade improvement.

But how can we reduce domestic demand? For practical purposes, only one course of action is open: cutting the budget deficit. Even if you don't believe the simple "budget deficit equals trade deficit" formula that Feldstein made so popular, there are no plausible ways for the federal government to make room for balanced trade except by balancing its budget. This might not work: Even balancing the budget might fail to eliminate the trade deficit (we'll spend more time on this in chapter 7). But it is the only plausible policy.

So the solution to the trade deficit is both clear and unacceptable. Eliminate the budget deficit and drive the dollar down (or impose new restrictions on imports), and probably (though not certainly) the trade deficit will shrink rapidly. But since we are in no hurry to eliminate the budget deficit, the solution isn't available. Implicitly, the United States has decided to live with its trade deficit for quite a while.

5   Inflation

The dramatic reduction in inflation in the first half of the 1980s was the great triumph of U.S. economic policy in the decade. At the end of the 1970s the U.S. inflation rate seemed out of control. In 1979, for the first time ever in peacetime, consumer prices rose at a double-digit rate (12 percent); in 1980 the inflation rate rose to 13 percent. Few would have predicted that by 1986 the inflation rate would have been just 4 percent—and that it would be only 3 percent a decade later.

Yet the victory was far from total. Inflation was stabilized, not eliminated, at rates that would have been regarded as unacceptable a generation ago. Public officials insist that inflation can and will be gradually eliminated. But in fact the inflation rate has changed little for the past decade. Even though inflation eased in the 1980s while the trade deficit went up, current U.S. policy toward both is much the same: to live with what we have.

Why isn't eliminating inflation a priority? For the same reasons that reducing the trade deficit isn't a priority: because the costs of living with inflation are not too high, and the costs of bringing it down look unacceptable. Given the diminished expectations of the American people, getting inflation down to the point where prices only double every 25 years is good enough.

The costs of inflation

Why is inflation a bad thing? That's a surprisingly hard question to answer. In fact, it is one of the dirty little secrets of economic analysis that even though inflation is universally regarded as a terrible scourge, most efforts to measure its costs come up with embarrassingly small numbers.

To see why, it may be useful to ask a superficially silly question: Are the British better off because they have such a valuable currency? The pound sterling is worth about $1.50 on foreign exchange markets. This means that, on average, the price rung up for any given item on an American cash register is about 1.5 times as high as the price rung up for the same item on a British cash register. Would we be better off if we made a dollar equal in value to a pound? Of course not. If the dollar were worth more, everybody's income in dollar terms would be that much less.

Now suppose that over the next ten years the overall level of U.S. prices were to rise by 50 percent (not a bad guess). Will this hurt us? Arguably it will do no more harm than deciding to use dollars instead of pounds to calculate prices. What harm does it do if all prices rise by 50 percent, if all income rises by the same amount? In real terms everyone will be in the same position, so nobody has actually lost.

That isn't the whole story, of course. But it is important to realize that to an important extent inflation is, as economists like to say, "neutral"—a general rise in prices need not affect anything real.

Where does the harm from inflation come from, then? The answer is that what really hurts the economy is not higher prices as such but the fact that prices are constantly changing, which can distort decisions and reduce the economy's efficiency.

The most concrete cost of inflation is that it discourages the use of money. In economies experiencing "hyperinflation" (that is, inflation at an annual rate in the thousands of percent), people may stop using money altogether, resorting to barter or to the use of black market foreign currency to avoid holding cash that loses value by the hour. This obviously cripples a modern economy. For an economy with inflation of 10 percent or less a year, however, the demonetizing effect of inflation is trivial.

More significant for the United States is the fact that inflation causes problems for the tax system. Inflation creates paper gains for the owners of assets that do not represent gains in real value— yet these paper gains are taxable, and so inflation may discourage saving and capital formation. On the other hand, inflation also creates paper losses for firms that have a lot of debt, which helps reduce their taxes—and it therefore encourages increased corporate debt, a phenomenon that worries many people.

Inflation may harm investment in other ways. In an inflationary world, accounting measures of corporate performance become confusing: some reported profits and losses are really just inflation illusion. Investors may therefore have difficulty evaluating firms in an inflationary world, and firms may have difficulty evaluating their own investment plans; so inflation may degrade the quality of business decisions.[1]

Lastly, unexpected inflation can produce windfall losses to individuals and institutions; even if losses are matched by gains elsewhere, they can be disruptive. The most dramatic example is that of the savings and loan industry, where fluctuations in the inflation rate conspired with regulatory blunders to produce a public policy disaster.

---

1. It is sometimes argued that fear of inflation discourages investment by keeping long-term interest rates high. This is half right. Expectations of inflation do keep interest rates high; but they do so precisely because borrowers are willing to pay higher rates when they expect to repay in dollars of reduced purchasing power. In fact, if we were to eliminate inflation—which would be a surprising development—the result would be catastrophic to all those firms and individuals who have borrowed long-term money at interest rates based on the assumption that inflation will reduce the real burden of repayment. So the direct effect of inflation on nominal interest rates does not systematically increase the real cost of borrowing.

All of these costs of inflation are, however, either small or avoidable. The United States does not, at its current inflation rate, run any risk of becoming a barter economy. The tax problems caused by inflation could be met with tax reform instead of lower inflation. Accounting standards could be revised to take account of inflation. And the costs of past surprises in inflation are mostly behind us. Any future surprises will come if inflation is eliminated, not if it continues at present rates.

As far as economic analysis can tell us, a steady inflation rate of 3 or 4 percent does very little harm—and even a rate of 10 percent has only small costs.

Why, then, was a victory over inflation so important? Partly because many people *think* that inflation hurts them. The costs of higher prices on the checkout line are obvious, while the role of inflation in allowing everyone to get bigger wage increases is less so. So there may be a public perception that inflation reduces living standards even when it really doesn't.

More important, though, is the difference between a steady inflation rate and one that is accelerating. In the days of Jimmy Carter, when inflation seemed to set a new record each year, there was a widespread sense that things were out of control—this year 13 percent, next year 20 percent, maybe the year after that hyperinflation. It was crucial to the credibility of economic policy that some kind of victory over inflation be won.

It turned out, however, that reducing inflation was not cheap. Indeed, it was almost inconceivably expensive.

The costs of disinflation

In 1980 there were many economists and politicians who thought that double-digit inflation was incurable. They were wrong. On the other hand, there were some economists, including the first

Reagan administration's advisers, who thought that victory over inflation would be cheap. They were also wrong. What happened was that the conventional *economic* wisdom, which said that reducing inflation would be very costly, proved right; but the conventional *political* wisdom, which said that these costs would never be paid, proved wrong.

How was limited victory over inflation won? Part of the answer is pure luck. In the late 1970s the inflation rate was swollen by a series of events that had little to do with economic policy. Most important, the fall of the Shah of Iran set in motion a temporary quadrupling of oil prices. Additional damage was done by soaring world food prices, driven by such disparate events as harvest failures in the Soviet Union and the disappearance of the Peruvian anchovies. In the mid-1980s, by contrast, the price of oil collapsed, and world prices of most other raw materials declined. To distinguish between these kinds of transitory events and more fundamental trends in inflation, many economists like to measure inflation not by the change in the consumer price index per se, but by looking at an "underlying" rate that leaves out changes in food and energy prices. When we look at this underlying rate, the late 1970s don't look quite as bad and the mid-1980s don't look quite as good. Still, the progress is impressive: Underlying inflation was brought down from about 10 percent in 1980 to about 4 percent in 1988.

There is no economic mystery about how this was achieved. America brought down its inflation the time-honored way: by engineering a sustained period of low output and high unemployment as a way of inducing workers to reduce their wage demands and firms to moderate their price increases. During the 1980s the United States, as a deliberate policy, put its economy through the deepest recession since the 1930s. If there is a puzzle, it is political: Why was the system willing to pay the enormous cost of this policy?

Recall the NAIRU. Any attempt to keep the unemployment rate below the NAIRU for a sustained period will lead to accelerating inflation. The converse is also true: To reduce the inflation rate, it is necessary for the economy to experience sustained unemployment rates above the NAIRU. Since a high unemployment rate corresponds to an economy running below its capacity, this means that to reduce inflation, the economy must sacrifice output.

Most estimates suggest that reducing inflation is very expensive indeed. To reduce the inflation rate by one percentage point a year, say the standard estimates, the economy has to run something like four percentage points below capacity. In another piece of ugly but useful economics jargon, this is known as the "sacrifice ratio": You have to sacrifice four points of output to reduce inflation by one point. That's a high price, even though the loss of output is only temporary while the reduction in inflation is permanent (unless you throw the gains away with irresponsible policies at a later date). It's hard to believe that anyone would be willing to pay the price of bringing the inflation rate down from 10 percent to 4 percent.

Yet that's what the United States did. Figure 13 shows the picture, which is about as clear as anything in economics. It shows two lines. One line represents "trend" output: a projection of what the U.S. economy would have produced during the 1980s if it had continued to grow steadily at the same 2.4 percent rate at which it grew from 1973 to 1979. This trend line represents a rough estimate of what the U.S. economy could have produced if it had been running at more or less full capacity. The other line shows the actual gross national product, which fell sharply below the trend line from 1979 to 1982, and did not get back close to the trend line until 1987. The gap between these two lines—the difference between what the economy could have produced and what it actually produced—represents a rough estimate of the cost of

America's war on inflation. This gap peaked at 10 percent of GNP in 1982 and averaged 3 percent over the seven years from 1980 to 1986. That is, the U.S. economy sacrificed more than 20 percent of a year's GNP to bring inflation down. This is a huge number: more than a trillion 1996 dollars. It is hard, in these pinched times, to imagine the U.S. government being willing to spend a trillion dollars on anything short of saving the planet, if that. Yet that was the price we paid.

There are two truths about the output gap and the war on inflation that need to be emphasized, because many people would like to deny them. First, the gap was not an accident but a deliberate policy. Second, that policy was bipartisan: Democrats and Republicans share the blame and the credit equally.

First, the deliberateness: The decline in output relative to capacity from 1979 to 1982 was the direct result of a tight money policy instituted by the Federal Reserve aimed expressly at controlling inflation by creating slack in the economy. Of course not every twist and turn was planned. There was a brief, undesired

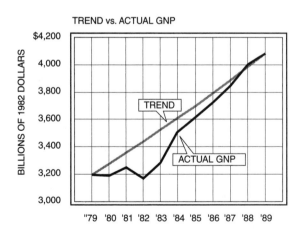

Figure 13
In the 1980s the United States followed a deliberate policy of reducing output relative to its trend, in order to reduce inflation. The cumulative "output gap," which represents the cost of our limited victory over inflation, amounted to more than 20 percent of a year's GNP.

recovery in 1981, to which the Fed overreacted, precipitating an excessively deep recession. But in the end the Federal Reserve got pretty much what it wanted. Using the old-fashioned, painful, but undeniably effective medicine of recession, it brought inflation under control.

Second, the bipartisanship: The policies that produced the output gap began in 1979, under Jimmy Carter, with support from both parties. In the face of near panic over rising inflation, Carter appointed a stern central banker, Paul Volcker, as Chairman of the Federal Reserve Board, and gave him a free hand to do what was necessary. The Reagan administration occasionally sniped at Volcker, but it too basically left him to do as he thought best. Democrats would like to blame the huge cost of the war on inflation on the Republicans; Republicans would like to blame the Democrats for the slump from 1979 to 1982 and take credit for the subsequent recovery. Neither party has a case.

In the end, of course, the war on inflation worked massively to the Republican party's benefit. The pain of rapidly rising unemployment came partly under Carter, and the rest came early enough in the Reagan era to be almost entirely forgotten by now. Meanwhile, the inevitable subsequent recovery of output and the lower rate of inflation helped lend a golden glow to the remaining Reagan years. This political windfall, however, reflected neither wisdom nor Machiavellianism on the part of the governing party, just luck.

What now?

The war on inflation did not end with a complete victory. Inflation has by no means been eliminated, and indeed during the late 1980s it crept up again, before falling in the 1990-92 recession. Will there be a second war on inflation to establish full price stability?

Some people think that there should be. The reason is not that the costs of current inflation are high—even foes of inflation know that they are not. It is that if we relax about inflation it will tend to creep up, and the whole struggle will have to be repeated. For example, Herbert Stein, who dismisses the trade deficit as a "nonproblem," declares inflation to be a real problem. Why? Because "if we . . . relax anti-inflation efforts now, what has been an inflation rate of 4 percent accepted on the assumption that someday we would start to get it down to zero will become a rate of 5 percent accepted on the same assumption and then 6 percent . . . Someday we will have to devote ourselves to getting the rate down, and the longer we wait, and the higher the rate we start from, the more difficult and costly that will be."

On the other hand, there are economists who argue that fear of inflation, rather than inflation itself, is the real problem. Robert Eisner, a liberal economist at Northwestern University, says: "Obsessions about inflation are major obstacles, more inexcusable when the overall price level is almost stable and serious inflation clouds exist only in the minds of those for whom these are perennial fears."

Views like Stein's carry immense moral authority. In an era when conservative economic principles command more respect than they had for half a century, and with the memories of double-digit inflation still fairly fresh, few policymakers would declare publicly a willingness to tolerate inflation indefinitely. Officially, the Federal Reserve insists that its goal is complete price stability.

This is, however, nearly pure hypocrisy. As the experience of the 1980s shows, reducing the rate of inflation requires high unemployment. Even on an optimistic estimate, to get us from current inflation to price stability over the next five years would mean maintaining an *average* unemployment rate for the next five years of something like 7 percent, not the 5.3 percent that

III   Policy Problems

Problems are not policies. While the trade deficit and inflation are the principal problems that worry American policymakers, actual policy is concerned with more specific questions—the budget deficit, interest rates, the dollar—that have a bearing on these problems but need to be discussed in their own right.

A description of America's economic policies is inevitably messier than a description of its problems. Policy is rarely a coherent response to perceived problems; more often it represents the outcome of bargains and struggles between groups who not only have disparate interests but also disparate perceptions of reality. It is easy to find examples of policies that seem perverse, or that work at cross-purposes. Yet the six policy issues examined here—health care, the budget deficit, monetary policy, the dollar, trade policy, and Japan—share some underlying themes. Each issue either has, or is thought to have, something to do with the trade deficit. On each issue policy has been constrained by fear of inflation. And on each issue both policymakers and voters have proved willing to accept a level of performance that would have seemed unacceptable a generation ago.

6   Health Care

Three months into Bill Clinton's presidency, his administration was the target of a strange legal challenge. A number of groups filed suit to demand that the deliberations of the special task force he had convened to develop a new health care policy be opened to the public. Up to that point, the task force had operated in extraordinary secrecy. Interested parties had noticed, however, that federal law requires public access to hearings unless they are restricted to government employees—and the health care task force was being chaired by First Lady Hillary Rodham Clinton, who was technically a private citizen.

The story was a nice illustration of the strangeness of American institutions, but the deeper moral involved the peculiar tensions surrounding the issue of health care. On other issues, the Clinton administration liked nothing better than to make a show of consulting the public; the "town meeting," during which the president took questions from ordinary citizens, was one of his favorite events. Yet health care policy, which affects ordinary people more directly than almost anything else the government does, was being formulated in what some people called a "Manhattan Project" atmosphere, recalling the secret effort that developed the atom bomb.

This was no accident. Health care is an incredibly sensitive subject, which one cannot talk about sensibly without treading on very dangerous emotional and political ground. Previous administrations had preferred to avoid the issue altogether. (The first edition of this book did the same.) Yet the need to do something about health care has become so critical as an *economic* issue that the Clinton administration felt that it had to move quickly to establish a policy. The probably vain hope was that by keeping the discussions secret, the dangers could be avoided.

Why is health care so important? And why is the subject so touchy? The answers go hand in hand.

The health care problem

The trouble with health care is simple: it has become incredibly costly.

In 1970, public and private spending on health care combined amounted to 7.3 percent of national income. By 1980 the number was 9.1 percent; by 1993 the number was about 13 percent. Rising health care costs were a major reason for the difficulty of controlling the U.S. budget deficit; the costs of providing health insurance to workers were becoming a major burden on the private sector; yet a growing number of Americans were unable to afford health insurance.

At a basic level, there is no puzzle about why health care costs rose so much. To some extent, the rise in costs was a matter of demography: older people require more health care, and the United States is an aging society. For the most part, however, the story involves the interaction between institutions and technology: an insurance system that couldn't say no, and a developing medical technology that played into that weakness.

Start with the basic fact: the great majority of Americans are covered by some form of health insurance. Older people are covered by Medicare; poor people by Medicaid; and most others by some form of private insurance, usually provided by their employers. Insurance doesn't cover everything, but it does cover most big expenses. So when a patient and a doctor discuss a possible test or treatment, they know that a third party will pay the bill.

Now suppose that in this situation there is a test or treatment that is very expensive but that might help a patient. A patient who was paying for his own health care might decide not to proceed, figuring that the money involved would add more to his future quality of life—or, if one wants to be grim about it, to that of his heirs—than the likely benefits of the procedure. But since he doesn't pay for it, he tells his doctor to go ahead. That is, the system does not make any trade-offs between medical gain and economic loss. In the jargon of medical economists, treatment is always pushed to the "flat of the curve": the point at which further expenditure brings no medical benefit, which may be well beyond the point at which a patient whose own money was at stake might decide that the medical benefits were not worth the cost.

This tendency to push treatment to its medical limits, irrespective of cost, has become increasingly expensive over time, thanks to the development of ever more sophisticated medical technologies. Once upon a time, there was only so much that even the rich could spend on medical care: aside from a few surgical procedures and some good advice on public sanitation, as recently as 1940 doctors had little to offer except a consoling bedside manner. Today we have an extraordinary array of possible tests and therapies: CAT scans and MRIs, radiation and chemotherapy, double and triple bypasses. These new techniques save many lives, and make many other lives more comfortable, but they do so at an often enormous price. The flat of the curve moves ever further to the right: we find more and more medically useful ways to spend more and more money on health care.

Does this mean that all Americans receive too much health care? No, because there is a paradox of the system. We will spend virtually unlimited amounts on insured patients, but not everyone is insured. And since insurance becomes increasingly expensive as it is called upon to pay for ever more sophisticated medicine, a growing number of people are unable to afford that insurance—a terrifying position, given the potential costs of medical care. The paradox is that because it tends to make health insurance more costly, improved medical technology actually tends to drive people out of our health care system. It's even possible that medical innovation actually worsens the nation's overall health, because the fancy new treatments do less good than the harm done when people who can no longer afford insurance are priced out of the system.

That is the basic picture of what is wrong with American health care. It seems pretty straightforward. Yet there is a mystery about the problem, which we need to confront before we can talk about possible solutions.

Why can't the system say no?

Let's restate the problem. When an insurer pays the bills, doctors and patients have every incentive to pursue any procedure that may yield a medical benefit, regardless of cost. This in turn makes insurance very expensive, prohibitively so for many people.

But there's a mystery here. Most people are insured privately, not by the government. Why don't private insurers offer "plain vanilla" plans tailored to those who cannot afford the current, expensive plans, or who would prefer to have a little less health care and pay smaller premiums? In principle, one might think, all that an insurer would have to do is impose some limits either on the kinds of procedures a policy will pay for or the maximum amount it will cover. Why doesn't the marketplace just say no to high medical costs?

There seem to be two answers. First is that while we have a lot of doctors in this country, we have even more lawyers. Unless one can spell out in excruciating detail exactly what an insurance plan will or will not pay for—and perhaps even then—it is all too easy to imagine what might happen to an insurance company that tried to offer a policy with more limited coverage than the norm. Suppose that the company refused to pay for some procedure, and then the patient died, or ended up crippled. Wouldn't the insurance company, or even the doctor who decides to limit treatment, be open to a very expensive lawsuit? The costs of medical malpractice insurance are legendary; fear of even more of the same may be one of the main factors making the market for health care ineffective.

There may also be a second, more honorable reason why we can't say no. Medicine is a huge industry, but it is not a business like any other. Doctors and nurses routinely make life-and-death decisions. They have traditionally been governed by an ethical code that expects them to aspire to a higher standard in their professional behavior than simply maximizing profit. While it is easy to be cynical, we all take it as a given that the medical professions will behave better on average than, say, used car dealers.

Now the problem is that an ethos of saving life, of doing the best for the patient—no matter how diluted by the fact that doctors are no more saintly than anyone else—is very difficult to reconcile with a system that explicitly provides radically different levels of care to different people. It is of course true that a billionaire will often manage to get treatments the rest of us don't, but that's very different from imagining a system that explicitly pulls the plug on people with $2,000 policies while keeping the machinery going for those who paid $5,000. A system that allows money pretty explicitly to buy life itself is, rightly, something we find hard even to talk about.

The result of this squeamishness is, however, that all health insurance tends to push toward the same norm, and that this norm is one in which even the most expensive medical technology must be used because it might do some good. Caught between the rapacity of the lawyers and the ethics of the doctors, the market for health care finds itself unable to control costs.

So what's the answer? The debate over health care reform often sounds impossibly technical, filled with complicated ideas expressed in dense jargon. But the essence of the problem—an essence that, as we will see in a moment, is too easily forgotten—is simple: how can we create a set of institutions that can really say no?

Reforming health care

Would-be health care reformers tend to come up with three basic types of idea. The irresponsible ones want something for nothing: they imagine that the problem can be solved by squeezing some set of supposed villains. At the other end are hard-headed types who want the United States to emulate the more or less centralized systems that seem to allow other advanced nations to spend much less on health than we do. Finally, there are the tinkerers, who hope that some clever rearrangement of the medical market can sharply reduce costs.

Looking for villains

When something gets as expensive as health care in the United States, it is a natural reaction to imagine that it is because someone—insurers, owners of private hospitals, drug companies—is profiteering. And without question there are some people and companies in the health care sector who are overcharging and exploiting the system. After all, health care is 13 percent of our economy, directly and indirectly employing at least 14 million people; without doubt it exhibits the full range of human behavior, from the highest to the lowest.

But can eliminating profiteering be a significant part of the answer to our health care problems? No: there isn't that much excess profit, and we probably can't do much about what there is.

A good illustration of the point came early in 1993, when there was a brief flurry of accusations of excess profits among drug companies. There is clear evidence that drug companies charge more for some of their products in the United States than they do in Canada, where the national insurance system uses its bargaining power to hold prices down. There is also some weaker evidence that the pharmaceutical industry earns unusually high rates of return, even given the riskiness of its business. On the strength of this evidence, President Clinton made several speeches lashing out at drug companies. But cooler heads soon prevailed. After all, even if the excess profits are real—a debatable proposition—they add only a few percent to the overall cost of drugs, which in turn are only about 7 percent of health costs. And how can we try to control drug prices without discouraging the research and development on which progress depends? In fact, the president's remarks had an immediate chilling effect on biotechnology stocks, raising fears that research and development in that high-technology industry would be crippled by lack of funds.

It is tempting to try to blame someone for the health care problem, but looking for villains is not a productive strategy.

Centralized systems

The United States spends more on health care, both in per capita terms and as a share of national income, than any other country.

Yet it does not seem to be healthier. Even if one discounts the special problems that come from our high rates of poverty and large
underclass, it's hard to see any indication that we are getting
much value for our larger investment. What are the other countries doing that we are not?

The most obvious answer is that they have some kind of centralized health care system, in which the government decides
how much will be spent—and that such a system is better at saying no than our decentralized system. This may sound paradoxical to people brought up to believe that free markets are always
more efficient than governments, but we have already seen that
the market for medical care is different from any ordinary market.
We have a system in which insurers and doctors cannot say no,
either because of fear of legal action or because they are unwilling
to violate social norms. Perhaps a government-run plan can
restrict access to medical care with less fear of legal action, and
can help to establish norms that are somewhat less expensive.

Centralized systems come in two basic variants. European
countries typically run medical care as a public service like basic
education: hospitals are run by the government, doctors and
nurses are government employees. Such systems are forced to
take cost into account by the simple force of budget limitations:
given a limited amount of money to spend, health care officials
must trade off one person's care against another's, which in effect
means ruling out procedures that are too expensive. The problem
with such a system is, of course, that it limits individual choice,
and is subject to all of the usual problems that can afflict a government bureaucracy. The U.S. medical profession has always
been bitterly opposed to "socialized medicine," but the system is
popular where it exists.

A much milder form of centralized medicine is the "single
payer" system that exists in Canada. Canada offers all citizens
health insurance, provided by the government; the government

sets rates and determines what will be covered, but people are free to choose their own doctors. It seems that this system is also considerably cheaper than the U.S. system, perhaps because the "single payer," the government, can set guidelines on what it will not cover that private insurers in the United States cannot.

A hard-headed approach to health care reform in the United States would be to adopt one of these systems, which do seem to contain costs better than our own. In practice, a national health service on European lines seems to be completely out of bounds for the United States, with its deep distrust of government and powerful private medical interests. A Canadian-style single-payer system is more conceivable, but the most influential advocates of U.S. health care reform think that they can do better with a novel system: managed competition.

Managed competition

The concept of managed competition is the brainchild of the health economist Alain Enthoven. Enthoven's idea begins with the observation that a growing number of Americans insure themselves, not with policies that allow them to go to any doctor, but via plans that limit their choices. Many people are insured with Health Maintenance Organizations (HMOs), which maintain their own staffs and require their members to use staff doctors unless they need to be referred to outside specialists. Others are insured with plans that do not maintain a staff, but that do restrict their members to getting care from a "preferred" list of physicians who have agreed to accept the plan's conditions on fees, procedures, and so on. HMOs in particular seem to be able to offer health insurance more cheaply than conventional insurers.

The "managed competition" idea is essentially to organize everyone into large organizations that will either provide health care HMO-style or at least bargain with doctors, drug companies, and so on.

Why might this help? HMOs certainly seem to have some advantages—perhaps because they are simply more efficient, but also perhaps because by joining an HMO an individual effectively gives that organization the right to limit the range of treatment she will receive. That is, one might say that the growth of HMOs is a way of providing something like the "plain vanilla" health insurance that we have seen is very difficult to write into policies.

But there is nothing preventing the growth of HMOs from occurring spontaneously. Why will a deliberate program of pushing people into large health plans improve the situation? And will such a program really deal with the core issue of stopping short of the flat of the curve?

The short answer is that nobody knows. Enthusiastic advocates of managed competition are very influential, but many health-care economists find their enthusiasm a bit puzzling; they can't quite see why rearranging people into big health plans will make much of a difference. The logic of managed competition is not overwhelmingly obvious. And since the system has never been tried, there is no real evidence on how it will work. A major study of the prospects for managed competition by the Congressional Budget Office, released in the spring of 1993, essentially threw up its hands and admitted ignorance: the idea might work, it agreed, but then again it might not.

I find myself among the skeptics. The essential health care problem seems to be one not so much of market structure as of morality. Economic reality requires that we place a price on human life and health, but that's a reality we prefer not to admit, and our unwillingness to face up to that choice explains why costs have exploded. It is hard to see how managed competition can resolve the dilemma. Indeed, one wonders whether the enthusiasm for complex schemes is not just another form of evasion.

Will health care heal itself?

In 1994 the Clinton administration finally presented Congress with the health care reform plan it had tried to concoct in secret. The plan was based on the general idea of managed care, but for a variety of reasons, including the ill will generated by the closed nature of the process (and the insufferable arrogance of some key administration aides), it was disavowed by most of the managed-care theorists—including Enthoven himself. Congress rejected the plan, and this ignominious failure set the stage for a Democratic rout in the 1994 elections.

While broad national health care reform seems to have failed, the private sector has to some extent taken matters into its own hands. Businesses that provide insurance for their employees now usually insist on doing so through HMOs that are highly cost-conscious. Probably as a result, health care costs have risen more slowly in recent years than in the past. In the late 1980s and early 1990s, the cost of health care typically rose at a rate about 4 percentage points above the overall inflation rate; by the mid-1990s the gap was less than 2 percent.

The problem is, however, far from over. Medical costs may be rising more slowly than before, but they are still immense and still rising. And while the private sector has to some extent contained its medical costs, the same cannot be said about the important fraction of health care that is paid for by the government. Growing outlays on Medicare, in particular, have become a central part of our next policy problem: the budget deficit.

It is easy, and perhaps appropriate, to become outraged over the persistence of the federal deficit. It is almost a decade since Harvard economist Benjamin Friedman, in a book entitled *The Day of Reckoning*, waxed eloquent over "inaction that would have seemed unthinkable not long ago: first the pretense that there was no problem, next the wait for others to make the necessary sacrifices, and finally the complacent conclusion that nothing could be done because nothing would be done." And still the deficit persists. If the apparent acceptance of more or less stagnant living standards is the most striking feature of the diminished expectations Americans have for their economy, the acceptance of a more or less permanent budget deficit is the most spectacular example of the diminished expectations the public has for its elected leaders.

Who's afraid of the deficit?

There are more than two sides to the deficit issue. Indeed, a minimum count is four, since both Democrats and Republicans are divided on the issue. On the Democratic side, one group claims that the deficit is a major problem and must be cured with a tax increase; another group claims that there is no deficit problem and new spending programs should be proposed freely. On the

Republican side, one group proclaims that the deficit is a problem (though not as bad as the Democrats claim) and must be cured by cutting spending; the other claims that there is no problem, although spending should be cut anyway.

Why worry about the federal deficit? There are two reasons. First, the government's solvency could eventually be in danger. Second, the deficit may have negative side consequences for the economy.

When the United States first began to run large deficits in the 1980s, worries about solvency were utterly remote. The U.S. government was not then and still is not anywhere near being unable to pay its bills, because it is easily able to borrow enough to cover the deficit. Nor is the federal debt, despite its inconceivable size, big enough to undermine this solvency anytime soon. At the end of fiscal 1995, after 15 years of deficits, the federal debt held by the public was still only 50 percent of GDP—less than the average debt ratio during the Eisenhower years.

In the last few years a number of voices have actually begun to warn about an eventual solvency crisis. We'll come back to those warnings in a little while. For most of the time that America has run big deficits, however, it was the side effects of the deficit that worried economists. The deficit, they argued, drains off an important part of our national savings, leading to a low national savings rate.

Despite periodic attempts by economists to raise public concern about the problem of low national saving, neither the idea of national savings nor the reasons why it may matter have been widely appreciated. So it is worth pausing to consider what national savings are and why we should care.

National savings

The discussion of national savings, like discussion of the budget deficit itself, is a political minefield. National savings are intimately bound up with both the budget deficit and the trade deficit, and therefore with how you read the record of the Reagan administration (under which those deficits emerged). That means that almost nobody approaches the subject without some kind of axe to grind, and that almost everyone tries to twist the discussion in a way that reinforces his political agenda. So it's important to start by getting the basics straight.

The first thing to get straight is that the crucial issue is *national savings*—how much the country as a whole saves—not the savings of any particular group inside the country. If I am convinced that national savings are too low, and you can show me that the savings of some particular group, like families, is fairly high, then I will not be appeased. I will simply have to find another culprit.

The second thing to get straight is the definition of saving. Saving means setting aside some portion of your current earnings to provide for the future. There are only two ways that the nation as a whole can save. It can use some of its current income to build more factories, improve its telecommunications, rebuild its streets and bridges, etc. That is, it can add to its stock of productive capital by investing more than enough to replace old capital as it wears out or becomes obsolete. Or it can buy assets from foreigners, either by investing abroad or by paying off debts incurred to foreigners in the past. The national savings rate is therefore measured as the sum of net domestic investment (increases in the capital stock) and net foreign investment (increases in the net claims of the nation on foreigners).

Since the early 1980s domestic investment in the United States has been slightly lower than it was in the past. Meanwhile, America has stopped investing on net abroad and started selling huge quantities of its own assets to foreigners. So the savings of the United States as a whole have been much lower since the 1980s than in the past. It's important to keep your eye on that ball. There are economists who will tell you that there really isn't any federal deficit, if you measure it right, or that households are actually saving a lot in indirect ways, and therefore that there really is no problem. Such arguments, however, have nothing to do with the measurement of national savings. They are arguments about *why* national savings are low. An economist who tells you that there is really less of a budget deficit problem than there seems to be is simply telling you that the causes of low national saving lie elsewhere than in the federal budget. Maybe he's right—but it still remains true that the United States as a whole is saving very much less than it used to.

Figure 14 shows how national savings as a percentage of national income has changed over the past few decades. Except during the recession years 1974–1975, the national savings rate in the 1970s remained roughly what it had been in the 1950s and 1960s—about 7 percent of income. Then during the 1980s the rate plunged to the astonishingly low level of 2 percent. Although the savings rate recovered somewhat in the late 1980s, it still remains far below its historical level.

The low level of U.S. national savings is particularly striking when we compare our experience with that of other countries. While the United States recently has been saving just 2 to 3 percent of its income, other industrial countries have been saving an average of 10 percent, and Japan has been saving no less than 18 percent.

What are the consequences of low national saving? Recall the definition: national saving is the sum of net domestic and net foreign investment. If savings fall, then domestic investment or foreign investment, or both, must give.

In America's case, the sharp fall in our savings was reflected in slightly lower domestic investment. The most dramatic effect, however, was the decline in our net foreign investment. In the 1970s the United States continued to invest slightly more abroad than foreigners invested here, so our position as a net creditor in

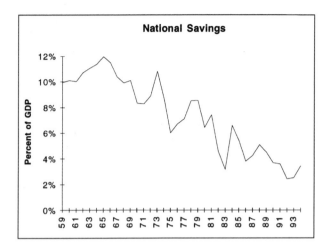

Figure 14
During the 1970s the United States continued to save about the same fraction of its national income as it had in the 1950s and 1960s. After 1980, however, national savings plunged to the lowest level seen in the postwar period.

the world economy continued to grow. When national savings crashed in the 1980s, however, the United States maintained its rate of investment by becoming a massive net importer of capital—initially by selling foreigners large quantities of bonds, and increasingly by attracting foreigners eager to buy controlling interests in American businesses.

The main consequence of the decline in U.S. saving, then, has been a growing dependence on foreign capital to finance our investment—the flip side of the unprecedented trade deficits of the 1980s.

Why are savings so low? There are two main reasons. First, as everyone knows (but some people choose to deny), the huge federal budget deficit means that the federal government is engaged in massive dissaving (or negative saving); that accounts for about half of the decline in saving since the late 1970s. The other big factor is a sharp decline in saving by households; as families reduced their savings and loaded up on consumer credit, the personal savings rate fell to record lows.

Nobody is sure why personal savings fell so much, or what could be done to increase them. Still, the important point is that the overall national savings has remained persistently at very low levels by historical standards, bringing with it an inevitable huge trade deficit. Since the trade deficit is widely viewed as a serious problem, why don't we do something to raise savings?

The answer is simple and has become boring through repetition: The only *reliable* way to raise national savings is to eliminate the budget deficit. Although some economists claim that reducing the budget deficit would do little to increase national savings, the reasonable citizen's view is still that a lower budget deficit is the one surefire route to higher national savings. Special incentives, tax reform, and who knows what else might help, or they might not. Eliminating the budget deficit will.

Apologists for the budget deficit

To the extent that there is an orthodox position on the deficit, within both the Republican and Democratic parties, it is the one laid out in the previous section: The budget deficit reduces national saving, helping cause the trade deficit, and should therefore be eliminated. (Where the parties differ is in how.) The deficit, however, has its defenders, on both the left and the right. While the mainstream of both the economics profession and the political community condemns the deficit, self-proclaimed experts have, with vigor and not a little glee, taken on the role of apologists for, and even champions of, the deficit.

The harmless deficit: The view from the left

The defense of the deficit from the left has come from a number of academics and journalists, but the most influential has been Northwestern's Robert Eisner, a past president of the American

Economic Association, and an economist with impeccable main-stream credentials. Eisner's argument, at bottom, is that the deficit is a statistical illusion. He rests his case on two points: the effects of inflation in raising the measured deficit, and the difference between the current and capital expenditures of the government.

The inflation point may best be explained by example. Imagine a government with a total debt of a trillion dollars, paying 4 percent interest on the debt, so its total interest bill is $40 billion. Now imagine the same situation, but with an inflation rate of 5 percent—and, because inflation tends to pull up the rate of interest, an interest rate of 9 percent. Interest payments on the debt will then be $90 billion, and the government deficit will be $50 billion larger than in the first example.

But does the government really do the economy any more harm in the second case than in the first? The government itself does not consume any more goods and services. Nor does the larger deficit encourage higher consumption: Owners of government bonds will understand perfectly well that the higher interest rate they receive is offset by the erosion in the value of the bonds

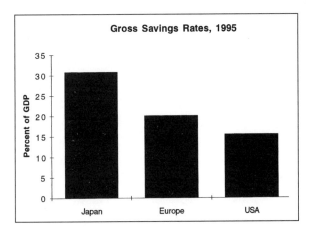

Figure 15
The United States saves far less of its national income than other major industrial countries.

by inflation, so they will not feel richer. So the larger deficit in the second case won't lead to higher consumption by either the public or the private sector. But since national saving is simply income less consumption, that means the higher measured deficit will not have a negative effect on national saving.

Eisner calculates that as a result of this inflation illusion, the national deficit of $150 billion is overstated by about $80 billion.

Next he argues that a good chunk of the government's spending is investment, not consumption: building roads, aircraft carriers, and other long-lived assets. One should not count this as part of the government's current expenditure any more than a firm's investment spending is counted against its profits. Thus Eisner concludes that there really isn't any deficit if you measure it right, and we should all relax about the deficit issue. In fact, Eisner and others argue that the really damaging thing is not the deficit but the attack on the deficit, which distorts public priorities.

What's wrong with Eisner's argument? The main problem seems to be that he ignores the context. First, if his arguments are true now, they were even more true fifteen years ago. At the end of the 1970s inflation was much higher than it is now. Furthermore, the attempts to hold down government expenditure since the 1980s have, by most accounts, cut the amount of government *investment* much more than the amount of government *consumption*—if complaints about deteriorating infrastructure are taken seriously, we may even have negative *net* government investment. So a calculation along Eisner's lines leads to the conclusion that under Jimmy Carter the federal government was running a huge surplus! Whether you agree with the measurement is less important than the fact that, however you measure it, the federal government moved sharply *toward* deficit in the 1980s, and thus contributed to the decline in national savings.

And here's where the second criticism of Eisner's argument comes in. Maybe there really isn't any government deficit, but we certainly do have a huge trade deficit. We cannot do much to cut this deficit unless national savings can be raised—and cutting the federal deficit is the only reliable tool we have to do this. So if you are worried about the trade deficit, what difference does it make if Eisner can show that by some measure we don't have a budget deficit?

The harmless deficit: The view from the right

While some on the left deny that there is really a deficit, an influential group of economists on the right argues that it doesn't matter what the deficit is. The leader of this group is Robert Barro of Harvard, whose professional standing is, if anything, even greater than Eisner's. Barro and his followers maintain that as long as the U.S. government is solvent—which it clearly is—the actual size of the deficit is irrelevant.

Barro's argument may be conveyed by the following example. Suppose that the federal government were to announce that it was reducing everyone's taxes this year, that it would cover the revenue loss by selling one-year bonds, and that it would levy a special tax surcharge next year to pay off the bonds. What would be the effect on consumer spending?

Barro says that there would be no effect. Everyone would realize that their higher income this year will be offset by lower income next year, and that they would need to put aside the current tax rebate to pay the higher future taxes. So, according to Barro, just about all of the tax reduction would be saved. The federal deficit would rise, but so would private saving, and national saving would be unaffected.

Generalizing from this example, Barro and his followers contend that changes in tax rates have no effect on national saving. If the government raises taxes now, the reduced government debt will mean lower taxes later, and people will therefore not cut their current consumption.

Does this mean that nothing the government does will affect private spending? No—but what matters is how much the government spends, not how much it collects in taxes. If the government introduces a new spending program, then individuals will realize that this increases the amount of taxes they have to pay— if not now, then later with interest. So they will cut their consumption immediately. The point is not that what the government does is unimportant, but rather that the decision whether to tax now or later, to run a deficit or raise taxes immediately, is basically irrelevant.

Although this view of the deficit is highly abstract, it has two key features that help raise an economic theory to prominence. First, it appeals to the professional instincts of many economists, who always prefer to push the assumption of rational economic behavior as far as possible. Second, it serves a political end: The Barro view, however honestly held by its academic proponents, can be appropriated by apologists for the deficit record of Republicans in the White House. As a result, Barro's views have come to be taken very seriously, both by his colleagues and by intellectually minded conservatives.

Unfortunately, there is nothing in U.S. experience since 1980 that lends empirical support to the Barro view. When the Reagan administration cut taxes without cutting aggregate spending, private savings did not rise—they fell. Moreover, Barro's theory requires that ordinary households be extremely well informed and rational about the future tax implications of current government spending—to a degree that seems quite unlikely. What fraction of the American public knows anything of substance about the federal budget? The notion that ordinary Americans can readily form reasonable estimates of the budget's implications for their tax rates over the rest of their lives strains credulity. In practice, one does not often hear Barro's views expressed directly in Washington's corridors of power. But they do play an important role in maintaining a climate of doubt about whether the budget deficit is really a serious problem.

The solvency issue

Until the early 1990s, demands to do something about the deficit were mainly couched in terms of the impact of deficits on U.S. national savings. Everyone took it for granted that any concerns over solvency were so remote as not to be a matter for current concern. But in the last few years there has been a gradual sea change in the debate: year by year the worriers have talked less about the macroeconomics of the deficit and more about the long-run ability of the U.S. government to keep its head above water.

On the face of it, this new worry about solvency might seem strange. Deficits as a share of GDP plunged during the mid-1990s, to levels not seen since the 1970s. Although the ratio of debt to GDP doubled during the 1980s, its pace of growth has been much slower since then, and it appears to have nearly flattened out at a level that Eisenhower-era America had no trouble living with. Why these new worries?

The answer is that a huge army is on the march. The baby boomers—that enormous generation born between the end of World War II and the late 1950s—are getting older. In the year 2007 a few of them will reach the age of 62 and take early retirement; in 2010 the first ranks will reach the standard retirement age of 65; and from then on the ranks of Americans enjoying their golden years will swell inexorably, reaching a peak around 2020.

This aging of the population will create huge, forseeable budget problems. It is only a modest exaggeration to say that the federal government is largely a machine that taxes working-age Americans and uses the proceeds to provide benefits to retirees. The numbers are fairly simple (figure 16). A little more than one-sixth of the federal budget goes to national defense; a little less

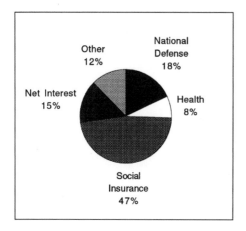

Figure 16
The bulk of federal spending goes for defense, social insurance, and interest on the federal debt. This makes radical further cuts in total spending nearly impossible.

than that to paying interest on federal debt. Of what is left, just about half is taken up by only two programs, both targeted on retirees: Social Security, which provides older Americans with income, and Medicare, which provides them with health care.

In principle, both Social Security and Medicare are run like private pension funds: people make contributions during their working lives, then receive benefits later. In practice, however, both systems have promised the great majority of people benefits that are much larger than their contributions. How is this possible? By the magic of population growth. To make things simple, imagine a world in which everyone lives for only two periods: a first period in which they work and pay Social Security taxes, and a second period in which they receive benefits. And suppose for a moment that the population grows steadily, so that each generation is, say, 30 percent larger than the previous one. Then by running the system on a pay-as-you-go basis, the Social Security Administration could pay out 35 percent more to each generation than it paid in: simply use the contributions of generation 2 to pay benefits to generation 1, the contributions of generation 3 to pay benefits to generation 2, and so on. (Actually, the deal can be even sweeter if average wages are rising, so that each generation is not only more numerous but earns more than its parents.) As long as the working-age population continues to grow steadily, this can go on forever.

Unfortunately, the working-age population in the United States has not grown steadily. It soared from the late 1960s to the early 1980s, as the baby boomers grew up; it has grown far more slowly since. And as the boomers begin to retire, the number of people paying into Social Security and Medicare will stagnate, while the number of people making claims on these programs will explode. The result will be a completely predictable budget crisis.

How big a crisis will it be? There are several different ways to put numbers to the problem, but one of the most dramatic is to recognize that by promising retirement and medical benefits to millions of people without putting aside sufficient funds to pay for those benefits, the federal government has in effect taken on a large additional debt that does not show up in the normal budget figures. And most people who have worked with the numbers believe that this hidden debt is as large or larger than the government's visible debt. One recent estimate suggests that the true debt of the U.S. government, taking account of Social Security and Medicare, is around 140 percent of GDP. That is, in reality we may be more deeply in debt now than we were at the end of World War II. And if you count in the interest the government would be paying on this debt if it were out in the open, the true federal deficit is more than twice as large as the numbers you read in the papers.

Of course, the United States managed to cope very well with the huge debt incurred while fighting World War II. There is no economic reason why we could not cope similarly well with our current situation. But we are not in fact doing so. In the first few years after the war, the federal government ran large surpluses; thereafter it had a roughly balanced budget, which meant that the fairly constant dollar value of debt became an ever smaller fraction of a growing GDP. In the mid-1990s, by contrast, the federal government continues to run large deficits—and these deficits would be much bigger if we counted the implicit interest on our hidden debt.

Or to put it in a more straightforward way: we know, as surely as you can know anything about the economic future, that 15 years from now the government will face a large increase in the size of its obligations relative to its tax base. A prudent planner would be saving for that day, running budget surpluses to pay off our current debts and maybe even build up a cash reserve. Instead, we are continuing to borrow ourselves ever deeper into debt. It is startlingly irresponsible behavior, by any standard.

But what will actually happen when the baby boom hits the budget? That is hard to say. One possibility is that the government will sharply raise taxes to pay for retirement benefits and health care. Typical estimates suggest that federal taxes would have to rise by about 50 percent to raise enough money, which would create a political firestorm. Alternatively, the federal government could renege on its promises to retirees, providing much smaller benefits than they would receive under current law. This would create an equally severe political crisis. Finally, the government could deal with the cash crunch by reneging on a different promise—its promise to bondholders to pay interest and principal when it comes due. But that, of course, couldn't possibly happen in America . . .

However you look at it, it's a scary prospect. The crunch is still a long way off—but we are now closer to that crunch than we are to 1980, when the United States first began running large budget deficits. Between the widely shared concern that the deficit contributes to an inadequate national savings rate, and the growing fear that unless we act soon there will be a real problem with solvency, you might think that by now there would be a consensus that the budget must be balanced soon. And indeed most politicians say that they are ready to balance the budget any day now. Why doesn't it happen?

The deficit deadlock

There is really no mystery about why it is so hard to balance the budget. The realities of taxing and spending mean that one way or another, middle-class voters must be called on to make virtually all of the sacrifices. But most of those voters have not yet grasped or accepted that fact, and few politicians are willing to take responsibility for explaining it.

To balance the budget, the federal government must either cut spending, raise taxes, or both. Let us consider each side of the ledger in turn.

As we have already seen, about half of federal spending other than defense and interest on the debt goes for Medicare and Social Security, both of which essentially provide benefits to middle-class retirees. Moreover, a good part of the rest also consists of programs that directly provide income to people that almost all voters regard as deserving recipients: veterans' benefits, government pensions, unemployment insurance, aid to colleges and college loans, and so on. Another large chunk goes to federal services nobody wants to cut, like air traffic control, crime prevention, and medical research, or that it would be hard to do without, like maintaining embassies abroad.

So what is left? There are some programs that the public greatly dislikes, such as foreign aid; but these programs are much smaller than most voters imagine. (In 1995 polls showed that the average voter thought that 15 percent of the federal budget went on foreign aid; the real number was less than 1 percent.) There are other programs that economists typically view as wasteful, such as farm subsidies. While these programs are expensive in terms of sheer dollars, however, they too are only a few percent of the federal budget—and have powerful political backers. The only other large chunk of money is aid to the poor—mainly the three programs of Aid to Families with Dependent Children (what most people think of as "welfare"), food stamps, and Medicaid.

One could try to balance the budget by cutting aid to the poor. And in fact, as pointed out in chapter 3, in 1996 programs for the poor were radically scaled back. However, spending on the poor has never been as large as the middle-class public imagines; even abolishing all such aid would fall far short of eliminating the federal deficit. The cutbacks of 1996, draconian as they were, were expected to save only about $10 billion a year—pocket change compared with the size of the deficit problem.

Realistically, then, any effort to close the budget gap by reducing spending must fall on programs that mainly serve the middle class—in particular, Social Security and/or Medicare.

What about taxes? Here the story is simpler. The poor have very little money, so they cannot pay significantly increased taxes. The affluent can be taxed more heavily, but only up to a point: if the government imposes too high a "marginal" tax rate, that is, takes too high a fraction of the last dollar an individual earns, this will have a serious adverse effect on incentives to work, save, and invest. And to make a tax increase fall mainly on high-income families, you must make taxes increase more steeply with income, raising the marginal rate. Indeed, Ronald Reagan, in the interest of lowering marginal rates, considerably lowered the taxes of high-income families. In 1993 Bill Clinton rolled back part of the Reagan cuts, significantly increasing taxes on the well-off. Most economists gave that tax increase partial credit for the decline in the budget deficit over the next three years. However, the Clinton tax increase raised the marginal rate for top earners to

40 percent. Even economists who supported that increase worried that any further increase might be counterproductive.

What this means is that any further tax increase could not be targeted narrowly on the very well-off. Like any realistic spending cuts, it too would have to fall largely on the middle class.

In short, any serious proposal to balance the budget must involve significant sacrifices on the part of many, perhaps most voters. Strange as it may seem, hardly any politicians have been willing to admit that—and those who have made a point of being honest about the budget have almost without exception been voted out by an angry public.

8   The Embattled Fed

The Federal Reserve sits in the middle of official Washington, three minutes' walk from the State Department, ten minutes from the White House. Yet psychologically it is a world apart. There are no lobbyists crowding the halls, few television crews outside, no "photo opportunities." The senior officials are paid more than their counterparts in the federal bureaucracy; there is no revolving door. Where the top four levels of the rest of the government are filled by short-term political appointees, the Federal Reserve consists of career technocrats top to bottom. It is a serious place, very different in tone from the rest of the U.S. economic policy apparatus. It is also, without question, the most powerful economic institution in the country.

What the Fed does

The Federal Reserve is what the British call a quango—a "quasi-nongovernmental organization." Its complex structure divides power between the federal government and the private banks that are its members, and in effect gives substantial autonomy to a governing board of long-term appointees.

The Fed's power comes from its unique role in controlling the nation's supply of so-called "base money"—the sum total of the currency in the hands of the public and the reserves that banks are legally required to hold to back their deposits. Banks can withdraw their reserves in the form of cash, or deposit cash with the Fed to add to their reserves. But the total quantity of base money cannot be changed except by the Fed's action.

By injecting or withdrawing base money from the system, the Fed has immense influence over the economy. Suppose that the Fed puts more cash in—which it usually does by buying U.S. government debt from a select group of commercial banks. These banks then find themselves with more reserves than they are legally required to hold. They lend out the excess, expanding credit and driving down interest rates. Furthermore, most of the money they lend out ends up being deposited back in the banking system, allowing a second wave of lending, a third, and so on. The result is that the Fed's injection of base money has a multiplier effect, expanding credit throughout the economy. The rise in credit and the fall in interest rates, in turn, stimulates the economy through a variety of channels: housing starts rise, the dollar falls (stimulating exports), business investment rises, consumer credit gets easier. Conversely, if the Federal Reserve withdraws base money from the economy, the process runs in reverse: credit contracts, and the whole economy is restrained.

What is important about the Fed's power to control the economy is how swift and technical its actions can be. Other kinds of economic policy take time and often legislation: tax changes and public works programs take years to craft. The Federal Reserve, meanwhile, can pull the economy out of a recession or (if it makes a mistake) push it into an inflationary boom, cool down an overheated economy or (if it makes the opposite mistake) create a slump—all with nothing more than an instruction to the open market desk in New York to buy or sell.

How should the Fed use this power? The answer its staff has always preferred is "with discretion." That is, they prefer to be left alone, trusted to do the right thing without any specific targets or guidelines. That's the situation they are in now. But they could lose it, and the Fed's struggle to keep its independence is one of the key hidden economic stories in America.

Monetarists, gold bugs, and rational expectations

The Federal Reserve, like so much of the country, was scarred by the Vietnam War, but not in the usual way. The Fed's sin was that when faced with Lyndon Johnson's determination to have both guns and butter, it failed to do its job. Instead of tightening money to keep the economy from overheating, it tried to hold interest rates down. The result was a gradual acceleration of inflation during the second half of the 1960s, from near stable prices to the 4 to 5 percent inflation that passes for stability today.

After a half-hearted attempt to bring down inflation during the first Nixon administration, the Fed did something worse: It allowed a rapid expansion of the economy in 1972–1973, which brought on inflationary pressures from the demand side just as the collapse of an attempt at wage and price controls combined with soaring oil prices to give inflation a huge push from the other side. The result was the worst inflation America had seen since the Civil War. Worse yet, it was difficult to shake off the suspicion that Federal Reserve Board Chairman Arthur Burns took risks with inflation to ensure the reelection of Richard Nixon—a suspicion without any solid evidence to back it, but one that nevertheless haunts the long memories of the Fed.

When inflation took off yet again, in 1979, the Federal Reserve's credibility was badly shaken. The Fed was soon faced with a variety of proposals to strip it of much of its autonomy. What made this effort particularly dangerous, from the Fed's point of view, was the fact that the opponents of an independent Fed had acquired a considerable intellectual cachet.

Since the 1950s, so-called monetarists, led by the University of Chicago's Milton Friedman, have persistently argued that the Federal Reserve, instead of making monetary policy, should follow a simple monetary rule. The essence of the monetarist argument is that discretionary policy on the part of the Fed actually makes the economy less stable, like a driver alternately stomping on the brakes and flooring the gas pedal. Friedman wanted the economy to be put on cruise control. Based on historical studies of the relationship between money and income, Friedman argued that if the Federal Reserve would simply ensure that the money supply grew at a steady rate, say, 4 percent a year, the economy would also grow steadily and without inflation. Between the 1950s and the end of the 1970s, Friedman's arguments gradually took root in educated opinion, changing from scorned iconoclasm to orthodoxy.

After Friedman came the gold bugs, a collection of conservative journalists and politicians whose intellectual clout was supplied by Columbia University's brilliant, eccentric Robert Mundell. The gold bugs argued that even Friedman's rigid targets for the Federal Reserve were not strong enough. A truly sound monetary policy would only come by tying money to an objective outside standard, such as gold.[2] In the 1930s John Maynard Keynes dismissed the monetary role of gold as a "barbarous relic"; yet by the 1980s the call for a return to gold had achieved widespread respectability, capped by a series of gala conferences jointly hosted by Senator Bill Bradley (D-NJ) and Representative Jack Kemp (R-NY).

---

2. A gold standard would be much more extreme than Friedman's rule because it would amount to fixing the quantity of base money. Friedman wanted the Fed to target "monetary aggregates" that included deposits as well as base money; he was aware that even with constant base money large changes in these aggregates could destabilize the economy. For example, at the onset of the Depression the supply of base money in the United States remained constant, but thanks to a banking crisis Friedman's monetary aggregates declined by a third.

Either a full adoption of monetarism or, worse, a revival of the gold standard would take away much of the independence of the Federal Reserve and shift its function from the making of economic policy to narrow technical issues. And that, of course, was the point. Both the monetarists and the gold bugs drew much of their intellectual justification from the influential doctrine of rational expectations. Loosely speaking, this doctrine holds not only that inflation feeds on itself via expectations of future inflation (a common view among economists), but that inflation could be cured quickly and with little pain if the commitment of the monetary authorities not to accommodate inflation could be made credible to the public. Tie the Fed's hands, said the enthusiasts—with rigid monetary targets, or better yet with a gold standard—and we will almost immediately have stable prices with hardly any recession.

The staffers at the Federal Reserve have never been monetarists, and certainly not advocates of a gold standard. They have always believed that their sophisticated judgment would outperform any mechanical rule. In 1979, however, with double-digit inflation, they found it hard to persuade the rest of the country of their competence. The ultimate success of the Fed in persuading the nation that it really does know best was a spectacular example of "judo politics": using the strength of one's opponents to win.

Volcker's victory

In October 1979 the Federal Reserve, under the leadership of Paul Volcker, made a dramatic announcement: Henceforth it would make the targeting of monetary aggregates its chief priority. Publicly, it appeared that monetarism had prevailed.

Three years later the Fed announced that it was abandoning its monetary targets for the year. Since then it has repeatedly done the same, and the targets have attracted steadily less attention. So the Fed, if it was ever monetarist, was monetarist for less than three years.

In retrospect, it seems clear what happened. The Federal Reserve was never monetarist. But it did need to win a major victory against inflation—both for the sake of the economy and to preserve its own treasured independence. It also knew that victory over inflation wouldn't come cheap (rational expectations had few friends at the Fed). The only reliable victory, in its view, would require a deep recession. The question was: How could the Fed persuade the country to swallow such bitter medicine?

Monetarism was the perfect answer. The Fed never said: "We propose to put the country through the worst recession since the 1930s, so that unemployment and excess capacity force the inflation rate down." It simply gave in to its critics and adopted monetary targets. Trying to meet these targets, not incidentally, meant putting the economy through the wringer. But who could criticize the Fed when all it was doing was what its most vociferous critics had been urging all along?

By the late summer of 1982 U.S. inflation was subsiding, but the recession seemed in danger of spiraling out of control. The sudden emergence of the Third World debt crisis raised fears of financial chaos. The result? The Fed cast off its monetarist cloak and returned to an active, discretionary policy. The money spigots were opened, and the economy began a rapid economic recovery. Subsequently the Fed has felt free to fine-tune—reining in the money supply when it fears a resurgence of inflation, pumping it up when the recovery seems to be flagging. In other words, the Fed went back to its traditional position that it knows best, and should not be tied down by someone else's rules.

For those concerned with the long-term independence of the Federal Reserve, the results could not have been better. The limited victory over inflation restored the country's confidence in monetary policy. The pain of the recession was quickly forgotten as the economy recovered. And despite occasional sniping from the White House, the Reagan-Bush administration had little to complain about: The pain came early in Reagan's first term, the recovery came soon enough to fuel a landslide in 1984, and it continued long enough to let Bush coast in four years later.

From a monetarist perspective, Federal Reserve policy after 1982 was nothing short of scandalous. The rate of money growth shifted erratically, sometimes rising to double digits, sometimes becoming negative. For several years after the abandonment of targets, monetarists—Friedman in particular—routinely forecast a disastrous acceleration of inflation and/or a severe recession as a result of monetary instability. Yet the actual result was remarkably smooth sailing, with both the inflation rate and the rate of GNP growth far more stable in the second half of the 1980s than they had been for a long time.

There are still monetarists, but they almost seem like relics now. Milton Friedman's forecasts of doom were at first taken seriously, then ridiculed, then ignored. The gold standard still has

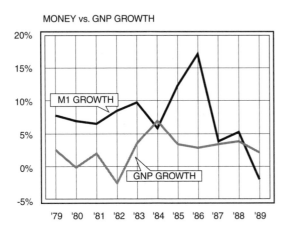

Figure 17
Monetary growth was very erratic after the Federal Reserve abandoned its monetarist approach in 1982. Yet output and inflation were remarkably stable.

friends at the *Wall Street Journal*, but in few other places. At the end of the 1980s the Fed was where it wanted to be: independent, trusted, and not too closely scrutinized.

The 1990–92 recession: A fumble by the Fed

Unfortunately for both the Fed and the country, the institution's reputation for overwhelming competence did not remain intact in the early 1990s. A series of miscalculations by the Fed's Board of Governors allowed the U.S. economy to slide into a painful recession; aside from the toll in failed businesses and lost jobs, this slump threatened once again to undermine the Fed's autonomy.

Economists are still somewhat puzzled by the suddenness of the slump that developed in 1990, in particular by an abrupt decline in consumer confidence. It was almost as if the American public took stock of the 1980s as soon as they were over, found the decade wanting, and decided that the time had come for some austerity. Still, the Federal Reserve has enormously powerful policy instruments and great flexibility in using them. Why didn't it manage to end the recession quickly?

One answer is that during the early stages of the slump the Fed's mind was on other things. In the late 1980s there was considerable agitation by conservative economists and their congressional allies for a U.S. policy aimed not simply at holding the line on inflation but at achieving complete price stability. The Fed wasn't prepared to launch another all-out war on inflation, but it was willing to contemplate some rise in unemployment, especially because many Fed staffers (and many independent economists) believed that the very low unemployment rates of 1989 were somewhat below the NAIRU. One Fed economist remarked to me at about that time that "we can't go out and create a recession, but we can try to take advantage of any little recessions that come along." This attitude probably made it difficult for the Fed to react quickly as it became increasingly clear that the developing recession was not a little one at all.

Once the Fed did start trying to stimulate the economy, it repeatedly overestimated the effectiveness of interest rate cuts, and was therefore consistently behind the curve as the recession gained momentum. With the benefit of hindsight, we can see that some of the usual channels of Fed influence were somewhat clogged by legacies of the 1980s. Monetary policy works through an expansion of credit; but many banks, overextended during the 1980s, were under pressure from regulators to be conservative lenders (see chapter 12). One of the sectors that is usually most responsive to interest rates is construction of commercial real estate; but over-optimism had led to a huge oversupply of offices and shopping malls. The Fed was by no means without influence—interest rate cuts still worked in stimulating borrowing through the bond market, in encouraging purchases of new homes, and in many other ways. The point was, however, that as the recession was spreading the Fed was repeatedly cutting interest rates too little, too late.

In the end, the usual policies had the usual effects. Output bottomed out in mid-1991. Initially growth was too slow to keep unemployment from rising, especially because productivity grew surprisingly quickly; but an unambiguous recovery was under way by late 1992.

The Fed as Scrooge

The economic recovery that began in late 1992 fairly quickly restored more or less the employment situation that had prevailed at the end of the 1980s. By 1996 the economy had added more than 10 million jobs, and by that summer the unemployment rate, which had peaked at 7.7 percent in 1992, was back down to only 5.3 percent. Indeed, the recovery in employment proceeded so convincingly that the Fed began quite early to worry about a revival of inflation, and in 1994 it began a series of interest rate hikes designed to prevent the economy from overheating.

This preemptive strike at a time when actual inflation remained low angered many in the business community, and this anger was fed by some economists who argued that the Fed's fear of inflation was outdated. MIT's Lester Thurow, in particular, pronounced inflation an "extinct volcano." This criticism of the Fed was reinforced by a sense that despite the recovery economic growth remained disappointing: the growth rate from 1992 to 1995 was less than 3 percent per year, and by 1996 this growth had slowed to barely more than 2 percent. Many critics in the business world and the media insisted that the Fed should aim for a much higher growth rate; one influential figure, the New York financier and pundit Felix Rohatyn, argued for 3.5 or 4 percent growth over the next decade.

Most economists believed, however, that this kind of go-for-growth position could be rejected on the basis of simple arithmetic. Although growth from 1992 to 1996 was fairly slow, this modest growth had been enough to reduce the unemployment rate by more than 2 percentage points. If the economy were to grow substantially faster over, say, the next four years, it seemed hard to avoid the conclusion that the accompanying fall in unemployment would also be substantially larger. The unemployment rate in 1992 was only 5.3 percent; to believe that the Fed could safely target the kind of growth Rohatyn advocates, one would have to believe that the unemployment rate could be driven below 3 percent—that is, not only much lower than the 1996 rate, but well below even the rates that prevailed at the height of the Vietnam War—without creating inflationary pressures. (Actually, if you took Rohatyn's numbers seriously, they seemed to imply that he believed in the possibility of a negative rate of unemployment.) Not many people were prepared to defend that proposition.

Although they were rarely willing to confront this arithmetic directly, members of the growth sect did offer some arguments about why they thought high growth targets are now feasible. *Business Week*, for example, wrote the following: "For some time, *Business Week* has taken a strong pro-growth position. We believe that U.S. productivity is higher than government statistics indicate and inflation is significantly lower. We see the global economy as severely restraining the pricing power of companies which recognize that in the current competitive reality they must generate profit by boosting efficiencies, not prices. In other words, we believe the U.S. can achieve growth rates higher than 2% without renewed inflation."

Many people found these arguments convincing. You had to think about them a bit to realize that they didn't make any sense.

Consider first the proposition that higher growth was now possible because true productivity growth is much higher than the disappointing official numbers. There were good reasons to doubt this claim—there is a lot of evidence suggesting that the rhetoric of business productivity has outpaced the accomplishment—but suppose that it were true. It still offers no justification for a more expansionary monetary policy, or a higher growth target. Why? Because estimates of growth and estimates of productivity are based on the same data. Suppose the official numbers say that the U.S. economy is growing by 2 percent annually, while productivity is rising only 1 percent. And suppose you think that the true rate of productivity growth is actually much higher, say 2.5 percent. Then you must correspondingly believe that true GDP growth is higher by exactly the same amount—that it is 3.5 percent. So you can't fault the Fed for failing to deliver a high growth rate: you must believe that it has already done so!

What about the argument that global competition prevents inflation? We might point out that the U.S. economy isn't actually that globalized: imports are only 13 percent of GDP, and at least 70 percent of employment and value-added is in "nontradeable" sectors that do not compete on world markets. We might also point out that if the economy really were as globalized as *Business Week* imagines, increased domestic demand would do little for U.S. growth and employment—most of the extra spending would be on goods produced elsewhere. But the crucial point is that if you believe that prices throughout the U.S. economy are closely constrained by foreign competition, it is hard to see how you can avoid the conclusion that changes in the dollar's exchange rate—which directly and immediately change the costs of those foreign competitors measured in dollars—must have a powerful effect on the inflation rate. An episode like the 1993–95 run-up in the value of the yen, which at a stroke increased the dollar costs of American industry's most formidable competitors by 50 percent, must surely have led to a sharp acceleration in U.S. inflation. But it didn't; and this is decisive evidence that global competition does not, in fact, constrain prices the way the growth tribe imagines.

A final point: a looser monetary policy would presumably lead to a weaker dollar. And if foreign competition constrains U.S. prices, this would mean that monetary expansion would translate into inflation more, not less, surely and rapidly in a globalized economy than in one with little international trade.

For these reasons, the great majority of economists regarded demands for a much more aggressive promotion of growth as wishful thinking, and indeed as irresponsible. These demands, however, continued to receive widespread public and political support, leaving the Fed under much more pressure than it has been in the past.

In the end, though, it seems unlikely that the peculiar institution of the Fed will be tampered with. Despite its recent fumbles and rough ride, it has almost certainly managed the economy more effectively than one could have expected from any more conventionally political organization.

9   The Dollar

The gyrations of U.S. dollar policy must often seem mysterious to even the most intelligent laypeople. Sometimes we like our dollar strong: in 1985 Ronald Reagan, in a widely quoted speech, pointed to the strength of the dollar on foreign exchange markets as proof of the success of U.S. economic policies. Other times we like it weak. In September 1985 Treasury Secretary James Baker, in a widely praised move, convened a meeting at the Plaza Hotel in New York at which the major industrial countries agreed to drive the dollar down. In 1993 U.S. officials more or less deliberately talked the dollar down against the Japanese yen, only to reverse course and talk it up again a couple of years later.

Through all these policy zigs and zags the economic experts have offered a running commentary that is even more confusing than usual, with some economists insisting that the dollar is grossly undervalued even as others argue that it is greatly overvalued. What's all this about?

To make sense of the dollar issue, it is necessary to ask what purpose dollar policy is supposed to serve. The answer is that we are trying to use dollar policy to help reduce our trade deficit. The reason there is so much confusion is that there are three unsettled points. First, are we really serious about reducing our trade deficit? Second, if we are, does trying to manage the dollar help? And third, if a managed dollar helps, where should it go?

Are we serious about reducing the trade deficit?

Arguably the United States has no real interest in getting its trade deficit down. As previously noted, our trade deficit does not really cost us jobs; the only certain harm it does is to increase our foreign debt, saddling future generations with the burden of paying our current bills. However, unless we are prepared to raise domestic saving, which basically means a sizable cut in the budget deficit, any attempt to reduce the trade deficit will come at the expense of higher interest rates and lower investment. There is a good case to be made that the United States should worry about savings, but not about the trade deficit.

Now we cannot run trade deficits forever. But, as Herbert Stein has pointed out, the nice thing about things that cannot go on forever is that they won't. Why not, then, simply rely on the market? A trade deficit poses no problem so long as foreign investors are willing to finance it, and it will correct itself as soon as they are not. So why have an active government policy of reducing the trade gap?

There are three standard arguments for such a policy, two economic and one political.

First, while trade deficits do always correct themselves, history suggests that the process is not always gentle. To take the most worrisome example, through the 1970s and the early 1980s Latin America ran persistent large deficits, which foreign investors seemed happy to finance. As late as 1981 the consensus was that Latin America could continue to borrow extensively for years to come. Yet in less than a year there was a collapse of financing that forced Latin American economies to cut imports by as much as two-thirds, plunging the region into a deep slump from which it still has not fully emerged. With the benefit of hindsight, it is clear that the governments of Latin America should have worried about their trade deficits, and taken steps to bring them down, while foreign financing was still easy, instead of waiting for the crunch.

The second argument, related to the first, is that reducing the trade deficit takes time. Firms do not change suppliers, or consumers shift to different products, overnight. Turning a trade deficit around often means building new capacity, new distribution networks, and so on. The U.S. experience with the declining dollar is illustrative. The dollar began declining in early 1985, yet the trade deficit actually continued to rise until mid-1987. If we think that the trade deficit will or should begin to shrink sometime in the future, even if the event is two or three years off, it is a good idea to start giving firms incentives to increase exports and reduce imports now. Of course, if the market could be counted on to be farsighted, if exchange rates and the investment plans of firms could be counted on to reflect a careful appreciation of long-term prospects, no special policy would be needed here. But nothing in recent experience suggests that markets are particularly farsighted.

Third, dollar politics cannot be separated from trade politics. The trade deficit feeds protectionist pressures in the United States. Unless that deficit can be seen to be declining, it may be impossible for an administration, no matter how free trade–minded, to contain those pressures.

So there is a case for having a policy of getting the trade deficit down. It is not a watertight case—reasonable people can and do argue that the trade deficit should not be a public policy concern—but as a practical matter the U.S. government does worry about the trade deficit and hopes to see it decline.

Hopes are not, of course, the same as actions. The orthodox recipe for reducing a trade deficit is to combine currency depreciation with fiscal austerity. The United States has been willing to try the first, but not the second. So we can legitimately ask whether it makes sense to try to do anything about the dollar until there are clear signs that a budget solution is in sight.

The answer is a definite maybe. National savings may be on the rise—even without dramatic action on the budget. That makes room for some reduction in the trade deficit.

Lastly, given the political dangers arising from protectionism, it makes some sense to take risks in order to keep the trade deficit down. The efforts to bring down the dollar after 1985 were condemned by all the predictable voices as dangerously inflationary; in retrospect things turned out just fine.

Yet, as noted in the last chapter, there are serious risks in putting too much emphasis on trade deficit reduction. In fact, the case for getting the trade deficit down is much weaker than the case for using a lower dollar to get there.

Dollar policy

The principal tool that the United States has to influence its trade balance is the value of the dollar on foreign exchange markets. The conventional wisdom holds that if the dollar's price in terms of foreign currencies can be reduced, U.S. goods will become more competitive on world markets, and the trade deficit will fall. That is why we had a deliberate policy of talking up the value of the yen in 1993, and why many economists and policy-makers argue that the dollar still needs to fall lower.

As in so many areas of economics, this conventional wisdom is under attack from both right and left. On both sides, it is alleged that reducing the foreign exchange value of the dollar is ineffective at reducing the trade deficit, and harmful in other ways.

The attack from the right has, as usual, more powerful support—notably the *Wall Street Journal*. Conservative advocates of a gold standard, which would preclude any devaluation of the dollar, are naturally opposed to the idea that changing exchange rates can do any good. They therefore are attracted to the arguments of such people as Stanford's Ronald McKinnon, Columbia's Robert Mundell, and supply-side enthusiast Jude Wanniski, who claim that:

(1) the trade deficit is determined by the balance between savings and investment, not the value of the dollar, so depreciating the dollar can't help reduce it;

(2) depreciating the dollar leads to U.S. inflation, which will wipe out any apparent gains in the cost competitiveness of American industry.

Like most appealing but wrong arguments, this one starts from some valid observations. The trade deficit *does* ultimately depend on the balance between savings and investment, and depreciating the dollar *can* lead to inflation that wipes out competitive gains. But since the exchange rate plays such a crucial role in translating changes in national savings or investment demand into changes in the trade deficit, it is odd to suppose that changing the price of U.S. goods relative to foreign by 25 or 50 percent somehow doesn't affect what we buy and sell.

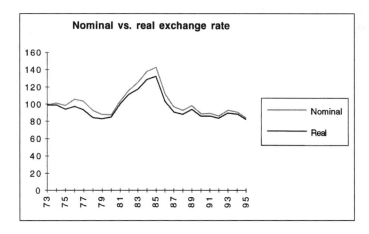

Figure 18
The decline of the dollar was reflected almost one-for-one in a reduction of the prices of U.S. goods and services relative to those of foreigners.

As for the argument that dollar depreciation just produces inflation, not a real improvement in competitiveness, this merely shows the perennial popularity of ideology over evidence. From 1985 to 1987, the dollar fell almost 50 percent against the West German mark and the Japanese yen. Did U.S. prices double? Was there even a sharp acceleration in U.S. inflation? No. In fact, the dollar's fall was reflected almost exactly one-for-one in a change in the *real* exchange rate—the price of U.S. goods and services relative to those in other countries.

The attack from the left focuses on a different issue: foreign trade policy. Critics of dollar depreciation such as journalist Robert Kuttner argue that it is pointless to try to reduce the trade deficit by reducing the value of the dollar. Why? Because our foreign competitors simply won't allow American goods in.

Again, the evidence on the whole contradicts this view. If the basic problem is that foreign markets are closed to the United States, here's what we would expect to see when the dollar falls: U.S. imports would fall because U.S. consumers would switch to cheaper domestic products; but U.S. exports would not rise because foreigners would not admit our goods. In fact, what happened when the dollar fell was just the opposite. U.S. exports grew very rapidly; if the trade balance didn't improve as much as we would like, it was because U.S. imports also kept growing. This suggests that the problem is not so much America's lack of access to foreign markets as its taste for foreign imports. (There is a caveat to all of this. We do have a problem exporting to one country: Japan. For the problem of reducing the U.S. trade deficit, this is only a partial obstacle, since Japan is only part of the world. But for American trade policy, Japan is a central problem, as we shall see.)

Can driving the dollar down help reduce the trade deficit? On this issue the conventional wisdom wins, hands down: Yes, it can.

How far is down?

The decline of the dollar from 1985 to 1987 had an unmistakable impact on the U.S. trade position. From 1981 to 1986, the volume of U.S. imports rose inexorably, while U.S. exports stagnated. After 1986, U.S. exports surged while import growth slowed. Indeed, from 1987 to 1991 exports from the United States actually grew faster than those from any other major industrial country.

Yet the results of the dollar's decline remained somewhat disappointing. After all, in 1980 the United States actually exported more goods and services than it imported. By 1992 just about all of the dollar's rise had been eliminated. Against some currencies, including both the mark and the yen, the dollar reached historic lows. Yet the United States continues to run a significant current account deficit: the 1992 deficit was $60 billion, and if the U.S. economy had not been so depressed, it might well have been as high as $150 billion.

There are two obvious, related questions here: Why didn't the fall in the dollar do more? And how far does the dollar have to fall?

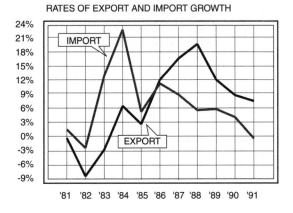

RATES OF EXPORT AND IMPORT GROWTH

Figure 19
The falling dollar sparked a U.S. export boom, but imports kept on rising, so the trade deficit did not fall as much as hoped.

The most important answer is probably the obvious one: The United States is just not as competitive as it used to be. Once upon a time we could sell our goods on world markets, even with a very strong dollar, because of our technical superiority. America made things nobody else could, and it produced goods known for their quality. Today the United States sometimes lags behind Japan and even Western Europe in technology, and at least in consumer goods we have developed an impressive reputation for shoddiness. So even though the dollar is back where it used to be, the United States is not able to sell as much on world markets as it was.

This is not a new development. The 1980 dollar was much weaker than the 1970 dollar, yet the U.S. trade position in 1980 was about the same as it was in 1970. In other words, although the United States was fairly successful at selling its goods on world markets throughout the 1970s, it was able to do so only because of a dollar that weakened steadily against foreign currencies. Apparently this trend continued through the 1980s. The falling dollar has been chasing a moving target.

It is a reasonable guess, than, that the dollar would have to be substantially weaker than it was in the mid-1990s to be consistent with eliminating the U.S. current account deficit. But how much weaker?

A rough rule of thumb from econometric studies of the trade balance is that it takes something like a 10 percent decline in the value of the dollar to reduce the current account deficit by 1 percent of GDP. If this rule is correct, eliminating the current account deficit that prevailed in the mid-1990s—which was more than 2 percent of GDP—would require a depreciation of 20 percent or more. Nobody would claim that this estimate is at all precise, but many economists would agree that the answer to the question "How far is down?" is "A pretty long way."

Should the dollar be driven down?

To eliminate the U.S. trade deficit, or even to reduce it to modest proportions, probably would require driving the dollar down substantially from its current level. Yet the recent trend has actually been one of a rising dollar, to some extent encouraged by official action. Why don't we make dollar depreciation a priority?

One good reason has already been pointed out. We aren't actually serious about getting the trade deficit down—at least not yet. The textbook recipe for curing a trade deficit calls for a lower dollar combined with a lower budget deficit. If we have no intention of actually cutting the deficit any time soon, then it's too soon to seek a lower dollar.

Other, less good reasons have also been mentioned: right-wing claims that a lower dollar would be both ineffective and inflationary, and left-wing charges that dollar depreciation is pointless in the face of foreign barriers to American products at any price.

There is one additional argument—associated with trade policy hard-liners like Clyde Prestowitz and Robert Kuttner—which we are likely to hear more of in the next few years. It goes like this: Depreciating the dollar is a bad way to reduce the trade deficit because it amounts to meeting international competition by cutting American wages, thus lowering the living standards of American workers. Kuttner, in particular, has derided economists who want to "devalue the dollar to the point where we are a poor country."

But if a lower dollar imposes too great a cost on living standards, what is the alternative? The answer of Kuttner, Prestowitz, and others is to rely on trade policy. Instead of lowering the dollar, they say, the United States should get tough and demand that foreign nations open their markets to U.S. goods. That way, the trade deficit can come down without the need to cut U.S. wages.

This is an appealing argument, and not without some merit. It is also quite misleading, in two ways. First, it makes dollar depreciation sound much worse than it is. When the dollar falls by, say, 30 percent against the yen and the mark, a 30 percent reduction does occur in U.S. wages relative to those in Germany and Japan. But this is not the same as saying that U.S. real wages fall by 30 percent: They probably fall by no more than 1.5 percent. Why? Because even now most of the goods and services we consume are made at home, and a fairly large part of our imports tend to be priced in dollars, too. Second, the idea that the United States can realistically expect to get trade concessions from other countries that would be an adequate substitute for a lower dollar is wishful thinking.

Yet the trade deficit, and the frustrations of dollar policy, inevitably put the alternative of protectionism on the table. And if the trade deficit grows, as seems likely, then protectionism is sure to become more and more appealing to many politicians.

10   Free Trade and Protectionism

When future historians list the achievements of the United States during the 50 or so years that it acted as the undisputed leader of the world's democracies, special emphasis is sure to be given to the creation of a relatively free and open world trading system. From about 1950 until the early 1970s, protectionist barriers to world trade came down steadily, and world trade grew rapidly. Nearly everyone thinks that this growth in trade was a good thing.

Yet there are now powerful forces in the United States working against free trade. Much of the argument for protectionism represents sheer interest-group politics: It comes from well-organized groups that are losing out to foreign competition and want protection, never mind the national interest. Yet not all the opponents of free trade are hired guns (and not all its supporters are disinterested, either). It's important to look at both the political sources of protectionism and its intellectual foundations.

The politics of protectionism

The basic rule of trade politics is that producers count more than consumers. The benefits of a trade restriction are usually concentrated on a relatively small, well-organized, and well-informed group of producers, while its costs are usually spread thinly over a large diffuse group of consumers. As a result, the beneficiaries of a trade restriction are usually much more effective politically than its victims.

The classic case in the United States is the import quota on sugar, which benefits a handful of domestic producers at a typical annual cost to consumers of $1 billion a year. This quota goes unchallenged, because the $5 average annual cost per person is so small that probably not one voter in 200 even knows that the import restriction exists.

But if consumers offer no effective opposition to protection, why is U.S. trade relatively free? Because *exporters* advocate free trade. Exporters by definition want access to foreign markets and are as well organized as import-competing producers. For the past 50 years the United States and other advanced countries have used this fact to provide a framework for maintaining relatively free trade. Trade policies are not set unilaterally; they are negotiated between countries.[3] In these negotiations, U.S. import restrictions must be traded off against the import restrictions of other countries, so that U.S. exporters become a powerful voice urging us to accept imports from other countries if they will accept our exports in return.

The source of new protectionist pressure is now obvious. When the United States is running a large trade deficit, the exporters who want open markets are outnumbered by the import-competing groups who want protection. If in 1980 you had told trade specialists that America would run trade deficits of more than $100 billion year after year, they would surely have predicted more, not less, protection than we have seen.

The relatively mild protectionist reaction so far is a tribute to the strength of free-trade ideology in the United States. The

---

3. The framework for these negotiations is usually the celebrated General Agreement on Tariffs and Trade, or GATT. GATT negotiations take place in a series of "rounds," of which the most recent, the "Uruguay Round," was concluded in 1994.

question is how long this can last. It may be useful to think of the United States as having a "protectionist overhang": a backlog of potential protectionist reaction barely held in check. Fear of this reaction is one of the main reasons for worrying about the trade deficit. If the trade deficit continues, sooner or later the persistent demands for more protection are likely to become irresistible.

But what would be wrong with that? Is protectionism really a fate to be greatly feared?

The (limited) evils of protectionism

Although most policymakers in Washington are convinced that protectionism is a bad thing, few of them have any clear idea why. In popular arguments against protectionism, the usual warning is that protectionism threatens our jobs—the Smoot-Hawley tariff of 1931, we are told, caused the Depression, and history can repeat itself.

Although protectionism *is* usually a bad thing, it is worth pointing out that it isn't as bad as all that. Protectionism does not cost our economy jobs, any more than the trade deficit does: U.S. employment is essentially determined by supply, not demand. The claim that protectionism caused the Depression is nonsense; the claim that future protectionism will lead to a repeat performance is equally nonsensical.

The real harm done by protectionism is much more modest and mundane: It reduces the efficiency of the world economy. To the extent that countries limit each other's exports, they block the mutually beneficial process by which nations specialize in producing goods for which their knowledge and resources are particularly well fitted. They also fragment markets, preventing firms and industries from realizing economies of scale. A protectionist country is usually less productive and thus poorer than it would have been under free trade; a protectionist world economy almost always so (see the accompanying box).

Just how expensive is protectionism? The answer is a little embarrassing, because standard estimates of the costs of protection are actually very low. America is a case in point. While much U.S. trade takes place with few obstacles, we have several major protectionist measures, restricting imports of textiles and clothing in particular. The combined costs of these major restrictions to the U.S. economy, however, are usually estimated at less than half of 1 percent of U.S. national income. Most of this loss, furthermore, comes from the fact that the import restrictions, in effect, form foreign producers into cartels that charge higher prices to U.S. consumers. So most of the U.S. losses are matched by higher foreign profits. From the point of view of the world as a whole, the negative effects of U.S. import restrictions on efficiency are therefore much smaller—less than one-quarter of 1 percent of U.S. GNP.

Other countries are more protectionist than the United States, and in some Third World nations wildly inefficient protectionist policies have caused major economic losses. Among advanced countries, however, protectionism at current levels is not a first-class issue. Without a doubt the major industrial nations suffer more, in economic terms, from unglamorous problems like avoidable traffic congestion and unnecessary waste in defense contracting than they do from protectionism. To take the most extreme example, the cost to taxpayers of the savings and loan bailout alone was about 10 times as large as the annual cost to U.S. consumers of all U.S. import restrictions.

If the costs of protectionism are so mild, why does the defense of free trade loom so large on the public agenda? Symbolism and politics. Ideologically, free trade is an important touchstone for advocates of free-market economics. As Paul Samuelson once pointed out, comparative advantage is one of the few ideas in

The costs of trade conflict

A hypothetical scenario may be useful for understanding what the costs of protection are, and why they are more modest than many people seem to think.

Let's imagine that most of the world's market economies were to group themselves into three trading blocs—one centered on the United States, one centered on the European Economic Community, and one centered on Japan. And let's suppose that each of these trading blocs becomes highly protectionist, imposing a tariff against goods from outside the bloc of 100 percent, which we suppose leads to a fall in imports of 50 percent.

So we are imagining a trade war that cuts the volume of world trade in half. What would be the costs of this trade war?

One immediate response would be that each bloc would lose jobs in the industries that formerly exported to the others. This is true; but each bloc would correspondingly gain a roughly equal number of jobs producing goods it formerly imported. There is no reason to expect that even such a major fragmentation of the world market would cause extra unemployment.

The cost would come instead from reduced efficiency. Each bloc would produce goods for itself that it could have imported more cheaply. With a 100 percent tariff, some goods would be produced domestically even though they could have been imported at half the price. For these goods there is thus a waste of resources equal to the value of the original imports.

But this would be true only of goods that would have been imported in the absence of tariffs, and even then 100 percent represents a maximum estimate. Our three hypothetical trading blocs would, however, import only about 10 percent of the goods and services they use from abroad even under free trade.

A trade war that cut international trade in half, and which caused an *average* cost of wasted resources for the displaced production of, say, 50 percent, would therefore cost the world economy only 2.5 percent of its income (50 percent x 5 percent = 2.5 percent).

This is not a trivial sum—but it is a long way from a Depression. (It is roughly the cost of a 1 percent increase in the unemployment rate.) And it is the result of an extreme scenario, in which protectionism has a devastating effect on world trade.

If the trade conflict were milder, the costs would be much less. Suppose that the tariff rates were only 50 percent, leading to a 30 percent fall in world trade. Then 3 percent of the goods originally used would be replaced with domestic substitutes, costing at most 50 percent more. If the typical domestic substitute costs 25 percent more, then the cost of the trade conflict is 0.75 percent of world income (25 percent x 3 percent = 0.75 percent).

economics that is true without being obvious. Politically, free trade is important as a counterweight to crude economic nationalism. So free trade has passionate defenders in a way that other, equally worthy causes—such as economically efficient environmental regulation—do not.

Even if protectionism isn't the most terrible thing in the world, however, it is still a bad thing. Or is it? While the great weight of educated opinion still condemns protection, there are some arguments in its favor.

Protection and the trade deficit

Arguments in favor of protection come in two basic forms. One argument wants the United States to use the *threat* of protection to extract concessions from foreign countries; those who use this argument are not advocating protection per se, but they are willing to use protection as a bargaining threat—a bluff that they are presumably willing to see carried out, at least occasionally. The other argument takes protection to be an intrinsically good thing, at least in some cases.

The bargaining argument for protection is usually stated in the context of the problem of lowering the trade deficit. The United States needs to reduce its trade deficit, say the advocates of this position; but driving down the dollar is ineffective because of foreign trade barriers and reduces American living standards. So let's instead expand our exports by threatening to limit our imports: This will force foreigners to open their markets and allow us to reduce the trade deficit without the need for a much lower dollar.

The main problem with this proposal is that it won't work. It is just not realistic to expect increased access to foreign markets to make more than a minor contribution to reducing the U.S. trade deficit, with or without U.S. pressure. The reasons are both economic and political.

First, the economics. When we talk about removing foreign barriers to U.S. exports, what do we mean? Despite the rhetoric, there are only a few major legislated foreign programs that have a large identifiable impact on U.S. exports; most of these are in the agricultural area. If Japan opened its rice market, or Europe canceled its agricultural support programs, this would help U.S. exports, but it would fall far short of curing our trade deficit.[4]

Meanwhile, there are political realities. U.S. pressure is simply not going to force radical changes in economic policy abroad. The major barriers to American exports are programs, like Europe's agricultural policy, with powerful domestic constituencies. American pressure may induce marginal changes in these programs, but it is a fantasy to imagine that by getting tough we can force other countries to abandon them. The U.S. economy is no bigger than Europe's, and not that much bigger than Japan's. Politicians in other countries answer primarily to domestic interests, just as ours do. We cannot expect to bully Europe or Japan into doing things our way any more than they could expect to do the same to us.

Given these economic and political realities, the proposal to use the threat of protection to solve the trade deficit will, in practice, inevitably degenerate into the implementation of that threat. To say that you favor using potential import quotas as a way to spur U.S. exports is, in the end, disingenuous: The result will almost always be fewer imports rather than more exports.

Indeed, however much they may talk about spurring exports, the advocates of a tougher trade policy seem much more interested in limiting imports. Robert Kuttner's own manifesto on trade policy, which advocates a broad system of "managed trade," takes as its model the Multi-Fiber Arrangement: an international

---

4. There is a special issue of access to the Japanese market, which is less of a matter of identifiable restrictions than of the whole structure of Japan's economy; we'll come back to that in the next chapter. But even if something could be done to remove the "structural impediments" to imports in Japan, it would not make a large difference to U.S. exports.

treaty that purely and simply restricts trade in textiles and apparel. That is, in the end he views protectionism not as a bargaining chip but as a permanent policy.

But what's so bad about that? We have just seen that the conventionally measured costs of protection are not very large. And there are intellectually respectable arguments suggesting that protection may, in some cases, actually be beneficial.

The economic case for protection

Economic theories matter, though not necessarily in the ways that their creators might have wished. In the 1970s public finance economists, Martin Feldstein prominent among them, worked hard to persuade the economics profession that flaws in the tax system distort incentives and retard U.S. economic growth. The result was to help create a climate of opinion in which supply-side economists could advocate radical tax cuts, leading to the massive budget deficits that Feldstein took the lead in denouncing. In the late 1970s and early 1980s a group of international economists— myself among them—similarly worked to persuade the economics profession that the principles of international trade needed to be rethought. This rethinking of international trade has won tenure and academic prestige for its leaders. But an unintended by-product of the effort has been to lend some new intellectual respectability to protectionism.[5]

Traditional international economics attributes international trade to underlying differences among countries. Australia exports wool because its lands are well suited to sheep grazing, Thailand

5. The "new international economics" is generally associated with several people: Princeton's Avinash Dixit, Tel Aviv's Elhanan Helpman, James Brander and Barbara Spencer of the University of British Columbia, and myself. The most widely read summary of the new ideas is a book I edited, *Strategic Trade Policy and the New International Economics* (MIT Press, 1986); an excellent summary of the policy implications is *Who's Bashing Whom?* (Institute for International Economics, 1992) by Laura D'Andrea Tyson, who became Bill Clinton's chief economic adviser.

exports labor-intensive manufactures because of its abundance of labor, and so on. The new international economics, while not denying the importance of this traditional view, adds that much international trade also reflects national advantages that are created by historical circumstance, and that then persist or grow because of other advantages to large scale either in development or production. For example, the development effort required to launch a new passenger jet aircraft is so large that the world market will support only one or two profitable firms. Once the United States had a head start in producing aircraft, its position as the world's leading exporter became self-reinforcing. So if you want to explain why the U.S. exports aircraft, you should not look for underlying aspects of the U.S. economy; you should study the historical circumstances that gave the United States a head start in the industry.

Why does this provide a potential justification for protectionism? Because if the pattern of international trade and specialization largely reflects historical circumstances rather than underlying national strengths, then government policies can *in principle* shape this pattern to benefit their domestic economies. As journalist James Fallows put it in a recent plea for a more aggressive U.S. trade policy, "Countries that try to promote higher-value, higher-tech industries will eventually have more of them than countries that don't."

Which industries should a country try to promote? One criterion is the potential for technological spillovers. Suppose that you believe that whichever country develops a high-definition television (HDTV) industry will find that its other industries, such as computers and semiconductors, gain an edge over their foreign competitors from their close contact with HDTV producers. Then it might be worth developing an HDTV sector—even if it requires a continuing subsidy due to costs that are persistently above those of foreign imports. This is an old argument, but it becomes much more attractive if the new theory is right, because the new theory suggests that the need for subsidy may be only temporary: Because comparative advantage is often created, not given, a temporary subsidy can lead to a permanent industry.

Another potential criterion for industry targeting has a sexy name: "strategic trade policy" (a term that is also loosely used to refer to the technological argument). A hypothetical example may convey its essence. Imagine that there is some good that could be developed and sold either by an American or a European firm. If either firm developed the product alone, it could earn large profits; however, the development costs are large enough that if both firms tried to enter the market, both would lose money. Which firm will actually enter? The answer may be determined by government intervention. If European governments subsidize their firm, or make it clear that it will have a protected domestic market, they may ensure that their firm enters while deterring the U.S. firm—and thereby also ensure that Europe, not America, gets the monopoly profits.

The strategic trade policy story (using the term to refer to both arguments) is not, at base, an argument for protectionism per se. It is really an argument for a limited government industrial policy consisting of carefully targeted subsidies, not for tariffs and import quotas. Yet it provides advocates of protectionism with a new intellectual gloss to justify their position, and it has been picked up enthusiastically by advocates of "managed trade" like Clyde Prestowitz and Robert Kuttner. If they do not argue that the United States should adopt a strategic trade policy, they at least claim that other countries—primarily Japan—have already done so, and that the United States needs to respond. As Kuttner puts it, "the New View radically alters the context of debate, for it removes the premise that nations such as Japan which practice strategic trade could not, by definition, be improving their welfare." There is a strong temptation for both politicians and intellectuals to run with this, to claim that all the old ideas about free trade should be thrown out the window.

In fact, however, few of the international economists responsible for the new trade theory has come out as an advocate of Kuttnerian trade policy. This is not because they are afraid to break the free-trade ranks. It is because the actual prospects for a successful strategic trade policy are not very good.

Once again, this is partly a matter of economics, partly one of politics. On the purely economic side, there just isn't any evidence that an aggressive strategic trade policy can produce large gains. Technological spillovers could be important, but they are difficult to measure. Take the example of HDTV. In the late 1980s there was considerable alarm over the fact that Europe and Japan had taken a commanding lead in the development of HDTV technology. The rhetoric of proponents of a U.S. HDTV program was almost apocalyptic—for example, Senator John Glenn described it as "one of the most, if not the most, crucial technological advancement" in progress. Yet others, such as the Congressional Budget Office, disagreed: "It is hard to believe that HDTV will . . . play a pivotal role in the competitiveness and technological development of the electronics sector." In the end, it all turned out to be a moot point: it soon became apparent that the technologies being developed in Japan and Europe, which transmitted pictures basically the same way as conventional television, were already outmoded in the face of new techniques that sent digital signals and relied on "data compression" to fit the information required for high-definition pictures within the limited bandwidths of existing TV channels. The point, however, is that reaching a practical consensus on which sectors really are strategic is certain to be extremely difficult —even without the interjection of interest-group politics.

As for the possibility of capturing monopoly profits through strategic trade policy, the result of a good deal of technical analysis of the prospects for such policy in particular industries over the past few years is fairly discouraging. The general conclusion of those who have tried to estimate the likely gains from strategic trade policies is that, while you can do better than free trade, the potential net gains are nothing to write home about—they are even smaller than the conventional estimates of the costs of protection. For example, a simulation study of the prospects for strategic trade policies in a number of British industries by Anthony Venables of Southampton University found that the potential net gains were generally less than 3 percent of sales.

Meanwhile, there is political reality to consider. Given the uncertainty about what strategic trade policy should be, wouldn't any attempt at doing it turn into thinly disguised interest-group politics? Almost surely it would.

The protectionist prospect

There is a better intellectual case for protection than there used to be, and the case for free trade is often overstated. Nonetheless, there is still a good case for free trade as a general policy—not as an absolute ideal, but as a reasonable rule of thumb. American interests would probably best be served by a world of free trade, with the temptations of strategic trade policy kept out of reach by international treaty. Unfortunately, that's not going to happen, for two reasons.

First, the other major players *are* engaging in strategic trade policy. Quite possibly they are doing themselves more harm than good. But it is extremely difficult to maintain a hands-off position in the United States when other countries do not do the same, especially when America seems to be in relative decline. The extent to which other countries are using strategic policy shouldn't be overstated, but the examples—Japanese protection of supercomputers, European promotion of aircraft—are too conspicuous to dismiss.

Second, the politics of free trade depends on a belief that market access is reciprocal—that open U.S. markets can be traded for open markets elsewhere. For most U.S. trade this has been and remains true. When we negotiated free trade pacts with Canada and Mexico, it meant increased access for both sides; the same would be true if we could negotiate a similar pact with Germany. But free trade becomes very difficult to sustain politically if there is a widespread and growing perception that one of the main players is following different rules.

The problem of relations with Japan—the second largest market economy, one of America's principal trading partners, but an economy into which the United States finds it difficult either to export or invest—is not the most important issue we face, but it is one of the hardest to solve.

11   Japan

An editorial page cartoon in 1987 showed a teacher addressing his history class. "Ironically," says the teacher in the first panel, "during the Second World War we were cooperating with the Soviet Union and fighting with Japan. . . ." In the second panel he continues, ". . . just like today."

It is easy to overstate the seriousness of the tension between the United States and Japan. When Wall Street economist Gary Shilling talks of a shift from Star Wars to Trade Wars, he is making a poor analogy: Trade conflict is a lot less serious than an arms race, let alone a shooting war. Still, the willingness of many American politicians to blame Japan for our problems, and the angry response of many Japanese to what they regard as scapegoating, pose a constant threat to relations between the world's two biggest economies.

Why are the United States and Japan so often at odds? In many ways the two countries have an economic relationship that provides great mutual benefits. Ask the Washington State loggers who sell their lumber to Japan at twice the price it would fetch on the domestic market, or the U.S. Treasury, which would have to pay far higher rates on the national debt if it were not for the inflow of Japanese capital; and, on the other side, ask Honda, which has half its market in America, or the managers of Japanese pension funds, who get a better return on U.S. bonds than they could get at home.

Yet there is a strong sense among many Americans that Japan is playing the global economic game by different rules from the rest of us. As long as the United States had a comfortable economic and technological superiority over Japan, complaints about Japan were limited to a small group, easily dismissed as representatives of special interests. But with Japan now rivalling the United States in many fields, the previous murmur of complaint has become a loud clamor.

Meanwhile, the Japanese view it all as simple envy and an attempt to make excuses. America's problems, they insist, are home-grown, the product of social disintegration, racial diversity, poor education, lazy workers, a pervasive emphasis on short-term gains, and a general intellectual and moral flabbiness. To the Japanese, U.S. trade complaints are an attempt to blame our own problems on someone else; their initial dismay has turned into growing anger—and playing turnabout, they are starting to blame their own problems on us.

Here in America, the lines are already being drawn. A 1989 *Newsweek* story on Japan divided American experts into "apologists" and "bashers"—no middle ground.

But what is the truth? A first step is to ask what is really true about Japan. Only then can we look for answers to the growing tension in U.S.-Japan relations.

The Japanese difference

Does Japan really play by different rules? You might think that this would be a simple question of fact, but it isn't. Instead, it is a source of bitter dispute.

The reason is that there is a wide disparity between the letter of the law and what actually seems to happen in Japan. On paper, Japan's markets are fairly open. Japan is openly and outrageously protectionist when it comes to agricultural goods—everyone knows about the prices of beef and rice.[6] On manufactured goods, however, Japan's tariff rates are about the same as those of other industrial countries, and Japan has few of the "voluntary export restraints" and "orderly marketing agreements" that limit imports of autos, steel, and other goods in both the United States and Europe. So in international discussions of trade policy, Japanese officials can describe their nation with a straight face as a leading practitioner of free trade.

There's only one thing wrong with this picture: If Japan is so open to the world, how come nobody can sell there?

By now, everyone has heard the anecdotes of businesspeople trying to sell goods in Japan—of firms that politely refuse to consider your product, even if it is better and cheaper than the local alternative, of retailers who will not distribute foreign goods. These anecdotes come mostly from interested parties, and they might be dismissed as sour grapes if the overall evidence did not bear them out. For the simple fact is that Japan spends less than half as much of its income on imports of manufactured goods as any other advanced nation.

It is important to point out that we are *not* talking about the fact that Japan runs a large trade surplus in manufactures. Trade surpluses are ultimately determined by the balance between domestic saving and investment. Japan runs a large manufactures surplus because it has a very high savings rate, and also because it *must* run a surplus in manufactures to offset its imports of raw materials. But it's not the size of the surplus that makes people accuse Japan of foul play; it's the way that surplus is achieved, with Japan seemingly a country that exports but does not import.

---

6. Although it is surprisingly hard to get Japanese to admit even this, I have had the experience of finding Japanese economists from the private sector refuse to acknowledge that the rice policy is costly, even in informal conversation. When pressed hard, they explained that they did not feel it was their place to criticize the government to a foreigner.

A revealing comparison can be made between Japan and Germany, the third largest market economy. In many ways Japan and West Germany before its reunification with East Germany were similar economies.[7] Both were high-saving countries that exported large amounts of capital to the rest of the world. Both were also crowded countries, with few raw materials, that had to run trade surpluses in manufactures simply to pay for their food and oil. And both ran very large trade surpluses in manufacturing in the 1980s. In fact, as figure 20 shows, Germany's trade surplus in manufactures was actually larger as a share of its GNP than Japan's.

But there the resemblance ends. Germany is one of the world's greatest markets for imported manufactured goods. The trade surplus came about only because exports were even larger. Germany simply trades more, in both directions. Whatever complaints one may hear about German economic policy, neither the

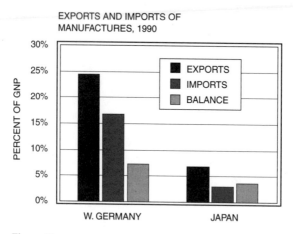

Figure 20
Measured as a share of national income, Germany actually runs substantially larger surpluses in its trade in manufactured goods than does Japan.

---

7. The German situation has been complicated since 1989 by the reunification of West and East Germany.

Americans nor their fellow Europeans accuse the Germans of having a tacitly closed market.

The Japanese and some of their defenders (like economist Gary Saxonhouse) will reply that the difference is geography: Germany trades so much because it is in the middle of Europe, while Japan is isolated at the edge of Asia. There is some point to this, though with modern transportation and communications, distance is not what it used to be. Even allowing for geography, however, careful analysis of Japan's trade volume suggests that it imports only about half as much as one would expect.[8] The businessman's complaint that the Japanese will not import anything they can make themselves is an exaggeration, yet the overall evidence broadly supports it.

But what limits imports into Japan, when there are only low tariffs and few import quotas? At this point the Japan experts get all fuzzy—which is probably appropriate, because Japan is a fuzzy kind of society, without the hard-edged legalisms that Americans, in particular, expect. Japan hands point to the inter-locking structure of ownership within Japan; to the long-term relationships between suppliers, distributors, and banks; to an economy that resembles an elaborate old boys' network more than the free-wheeling markets of America (and which is rife with practices that would be illegal under U.S. antitrust law). For any outsider, this economic structure is hard to break into; for foreigners, it is particularly difficult.

Some foreign experts like to view the Japanese system as not just closed but conspiratorial, tacitly directed by top officials at the Ministry of International Trade and Industry (MITI) and the Ministry of Finance. This is the view advanced by such bashers as Clyde Prestowitz, whose book *Trading Places* portrays a systematic

---

8. The decisive salvo in the academic debate was a 1987 paper on Japanese imports by Robert Lawrence of the Brookings Institution, which showed to the satisfaction of many economists that Japan really does have unexpectedly small imports. It is a measure of the growing polarization in the U.S. debate that *Newsweek* classes Lawrence, who has been an active crusader for free trade, as a "basher."

Japanese pursuit of strategic advantage at America's expense. It is also a view that is increasingly out of date.

There is no question that before the early 1970s the Japanese system was heavily directed from the top, with MITI and the Ministry of Finance influencing the allocation of credit and foreign exchange in an effort to push the economy where they liked. For a long time, however, Japanese firms have had plenty of cash on hand, both foreign and domestic, and a correspondingly greater ability to ignore suggestions from above. Old habits of deference to central authority are still around, but the still popular image of a centralized "Japan Inc." is at least 20 years behind the times. Fashionable current descriptions of Japan, like the books of Karel van Wolferen, depict an economy that is characterized neither by free competition nor by central direction, but rather by a web of personal ties and long-term understandings—a conspiracy, if you like, but one without leaders.

Even if there are no central strategists, however, the Japanese economy often appears to be following the very type of strategic trade policy that some Americans would like to see adopted here.

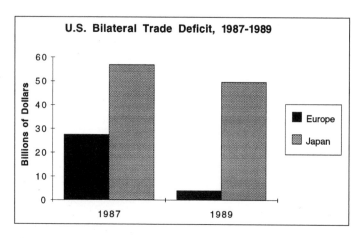

Figure 21
The dollar's fall, which helped the United States to cut its trade deficit with Europe, had little impact on its deficit with Japan.

The ranks of Japanese firms seem to close most strongly against imports of goods that embody new technologies, like supercomputers or what is known in electronics jargon as "amorphous materials." When imports into Japan do increase, as they did after the yen began to rise in 1985, they tend to be either unsophisticated goods or products of the overseas affiliates of Japanese firms, and not the kinds of goods that American firms think they should be able to sell. It is revealing that the falling dollar had a marked effect in shrinking the U.S. trade deficit with Europe but hardly any effect on our deficit with Japan, even though the dollar fell more against the yen than against any other currency.

In sum, then, the widespread perception that Japan plays by different rules is basically right. This is not a moral judgment; it's not a question of what's right or what's fair. It is just a statement of fact. Japan's market is not open to foreigners in the way that U.S. or German markets are open.

Corporate taxation and foreign direct investment

Somewhat surprisingly, the tax reform of 1986, which, in effect, increased the rate of taxation on corporations, may have been one of the factors that led to a shift of Japanese investment away from passive portfolio investments and toward the direct acquisition of U.S. firms.

In 1981, the United States offered generous depreciation allowances that cut effective corporate tax rates sharply. Somewhat paradoxically, this acted as a disincentive for Japanese firms to own U.S. corporations. When a Japanese firm owns a U.S. corporation, it must eventually pay taxes to the Japanese government on any profits its subsidiary sends home—with a credit for taxes paid to the U.S. government. This meant that Japanese-owned firms, unlike U.S.-owned firms, could not realize the full benefits of the lower tax rate, since the gain from the lower tax rate here was partially offset by the reduced tax credit at home. Thus the low corporate tax rates of 1981–86 had the effect of making corporations more valuable in U.S. than in Japanese hands.

The 1986 tax reform, which raised the effective corporate tax rate, eliminated this bias toward domestic ownership, and may therefore have played a role in the surge of Japanese acquisitions of U.S. firms that followed.

The Japanese are coming!

As trade conflict between the United States and Japan grew in the
mid-1980s, U.S. officials tried to buy time, hoping that a fall in
the dollar eventually would take the pressure off. As it turned
out, however, the lower dollar, while quite effective elsewhere,
had virtually no effect on U.S.-Japan trade. And partly as a result,
a new source of tension arose: Japanese direct investment in the
United States.

Japan has been investing heavily abroad, largely in the United
States, since 1982—a net capital outflow that is the inevitable
counterpart of Japan's balance-of-payments surpluses. Until 1986,
the Japanese characteristically put their money into "portfolio"
investments that yielded income but not control: Treasury bills,
corporate paper, and minority stock positions. Then, for reasons
that are still controversial, they changed their approach. Even as
the overall rate of Japanese investment abroad tapered off, more
and more of it took the form of foreign direct investment: investment aimed at establishing operational control. The purchase of
Columbia Pictures by Sony made headlines, but it was just one
conspicuous example of a broad surge.

The numbers show the surge clearly. In 1985, Japan parked
three-quarters of its foreign investment in passive sources of
income; by 1989 two-thirds of its investment flows were used to
acquire or extend control. The United States, as the world's leading capital importer, provided the counterpart: Where in the early
days of our trade deficit we were able to finance it mostly by selling debt, by the late 1980s we were selling whole firms. Many of
these sales were to countries other than Japan—British direct
investment is still larger than that of Japan—but Japanese firms in
the United States grew rapidly.

Why did this happen so suddenly? One reason is the fall in the
dollar, which has made the cash resources of Japanese firms look

large relative to the prices of U.S. firms. The tax reform act of 1986 may also have inadvertently opened the floodgates. (See box, page 141.) Also, sheer herd instinct may have played a role: Once a few Japanese firms had shown the way, others rushed to follow.

The more important question is whether it was anything to worry about. Twenty years ago, when U.S. multinational corporations were growing in Europe, many Europeans feared that the "American challenge" would overwhelm them. In the end, U.S. investment in Europe did not grow without limit, and U.S. firms in Europe soon came to be regarded as perfectly acceptable corporate citizens. Wouldn't the same turn out to be true of Japanese firms in the United States?

Well, maybe. But here as elsewhere Japan looked different, enough so to cause some worries. If you wanted to find cause for alarm about the Japanese invasion, there were two facts that can give the complacent pause. First, while Japanese firms invest abroad, Japan itself seems to be a very hard place in which to invest—so Japanese firms may have a strategic advantage over their foreign rivals in the form of a protected home base. Second,

COMPOSITION OF JAPANESE INVESTMENT FLOW

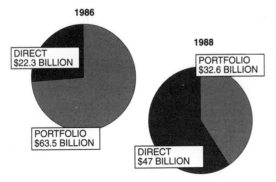

Figure 22
Since 1986 Japan has increasingly used its accumulation of assets abroad not simply to yield returns but also to buy control.

Japanese firms in the United States appear to behave differently from other firms.

The apparent inability of foreign firms to operate on a large scale in Japan is an even more striking fact than Japan's resistance to imports. Figure 23 compares the role of foreign-owned firms in Japan with their role in other advanced countries. Europeans have long been accustomed to the idea of working for foreign employers, having a substantial part of the capital stock foreign-owned, and so on; with growing foreign direct investment in the United States, America increasingly looks similar. But Japan is barely touched by foreign firms.

Japan's situation with regard to direct investment is like its situation with regard to imports, only more so. *De jure,* Japan is wide open; while the government does have some power to block foreign investments, that power is rarely used. *De facto,* foreign firms in Japan face endless informal obstacles.

The point is that with Japan now one of the world's great economic powers, the asymmetry of access—Japanese firms can invest abroad, but foreign firms find it difficult to invest in

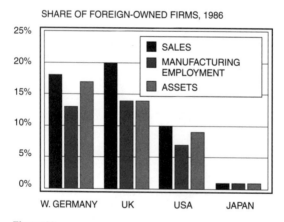

Figure 23
Foreign-owned firms now play an important role in all major industrial countries–except Japan, where their role remains of minimal importance.

Japan—gives firms of Japanese origin a kind of strategic advantage that is not negligible.

But what difference does it make? Why not accept Japanese firms abroad?

The first wave of Japanese direct investment in the United States saw the creation of manufacturing subsidiaries—first in color televisions, then in autos. To optimists, these investments seemed a clear plus from an American point of view: new plants, new jobs, domestic production in place of imports. Admittedly, there was always a concern that Japanese production would displace domestic autos instead of imports; but on the whole most people looked favorably on these "greenfield" investments.

The wave of investment since 1986 has not, however, followed this earlier model. The Japanese have not for the most part been building new plants. Instead, they have been acquiring existing U.S. enterprises. Bridgestone, a Japanese firm, bought Firestone; Sony bought Columbia Pictures. When a Japanese firm buys an existing American firm, we have to ask whether that firm will be run differently, and if so, whether the U.S. economy will be hurt or helped by the difference.

The optimistic view is that the Japanese will buy firms that they know they can run better than the original management, and so the result will be an increase in efficiency. The Japanese auto companies have shown that they can run plants in the United States at Japanese levels of productivity, raising the efficiency of the U.S. labor force both directly and by shaming Detroit into doing better. Surely they will do the same in other industries, and to that extent will help the U.S. economy (although whether Japanese firms can improve the management of the motion picture industry is fairly doubtful).

The pessimistic view is that the Japanese will rearrange their firms to suit Japanese interests, at U.S. expense. Prestowitz and Robert Reich predict that the Japanese will keep the high-wage

activities, the R&D, and much of the sourcing of parts in Japan.
The United States, in this view, will be left with "screwdriver"
plants where low-wage American workers assemble Japanese
products.

Since the great wave of Japanese investment is so recent, it is
too early to tell how it will turn out. The behavior of the Japanese
firms already here, however, suggests that they are innocent of
two of the charges, but guilty of the third. As figure 24 shows,
Japanese firms already here actually pay wages as high or higher
than both American firms and other foreign firms in the United
States; they also do just as much R&D. Unfortunately, the third
charge is true: Japanese firms do seem to import a lot more, most
of it presumably from Japanese suppliers, than either U.S. firms or
other foreign firms. On average, foreign firms in the United States
import more than twice as much per worker as American firms;
Japanese firms import well over twice as much as the average foreign firm.

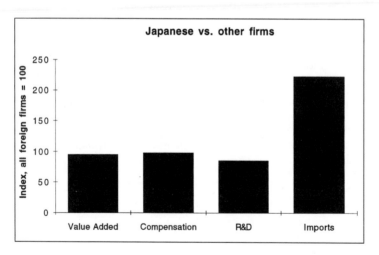

Figure 24
Japanese-owned firms in the United States look similar to U.S. owned firms and
firms owned by other countries in terms of value-added per worker, wages, and
spending on R&D. However, they have a much higher tendency to buy inputs from
abroad.

It is possible to make excuses for this high propensity to
import. In particular, the imports of Japanese subsidiaries may
reflect their sheer newness, the lack of time to build up a local
supply network. On the other hand, a tendency to buy from their
regular suppliers, even when it might be cheaper to source locally,
is just what one would expect given the other things we know
about Japanese industry. (Some recent comparisons of the behavior of Japanese firms in Australia with those from other countries
reveal the same Japanese reluctance to buy either locally or on
the world market.)

So here is the case against Japanese multinationals, if you want
to make it: They have a strategic advantage against the rest of the
world because of their protected home base, and they use this
advantage to pursue a buy-Japanese policy even when they
acquire production facilities abroad. Perhaps the advantages of
attracting Japanese firms outweigh these complaints. But in the
highly charged atmosphere of the 1990s it is inevitable that
Japanese investment will draw the same kind of lightning as
Japanese trade—and perhaps more so.

How much of a problem is it?

During the 1970s it was popular for radicals both in the Third
World and in the United States to blame the industrial nations,
and America in particular, for the backwardness of the rest of the
world. Someone once wrote of these radicals that they seemed to
see America as a kind of spacecraft, shooting death rays at the
Third World's economy. Few people would now portray the
United States that way, but that is the way Americans seem to
view Japan.

How much of a problem does "the Japanese difference" pose
for the United States? To defenders of Japan, and to those who
believe that a restructured American economy is about to enter

a golden age, there is no problem at all. To alarmists like Prestowitz, Japan's challenge is undermining America's economic prospects. The reality is more mundane. The Japanese difference hurts the American economy, but only a little. If our prospects are not too good, the fault lies not in Tokyo but in Washington and New York. The Japan problem is real, but it is not central.

The reason is simple. The main thing that matters for American living standards is still our own productivity. Foreign trade and foreign competition can only make a difference at the margin. If Japan's economy were more open, if Japanese firms abroad were better local citizens, we might be able to trade U.S. goods and services for imports at better terms. Our real income would therefore be higher. But it would be only a marginal improvement. The reasons for our disappointing economic performance lie overwhelmingly in our own shortcomings.

The flip side is also true: Japan's successes did not in any important way rest on predatory behavior against the rest of the world. Japan saves six times as high a fraction of its income as the United States and educates its children better than we do. This year Japanese industry will invest more in total than U.S. industry, even though Japan has only half our population. These are sufficient reasons for Japan to grow far faster than the United States, whatever our trading relations. Indeed, it is worth remembering that Japan's economy is not, popular myth to the contrary, primarily an export machine: Japan exports only 14 percent of what it produces, less than any other major industrial country except the United States. It is no wonder that the Japanese are scornful of Americans who want to claim that Japan's success is somehow "stolen" at America's expense.

So it is important to keep a sense of perspective about the Japan problem. Japan is not our nemesis. Japan's success hurts our pride far more than it hurts our standard of living.

Yet there is still a Japan problem. Japan is a great economic power that does not play by the same rules as the other great economic powers. Economically and, above all, politically, that is a fact that cannot be ignored. One way or another, the United States has got to find a way of dealing with Japan.

What to do

There are two extreme views about what to do about Japan. On one side are the old-time free traders, who want us in effect to turn the other cheek. On the other side are the bashers, who want us to confront Japan and demand massive change, or else. So emotional has the dispute between these factions become that it has descended to the level of *ad hominem* charges—free traders accused of getting money from the Japanese, bashers accused of getting money from protectionist special interests. But let's look at the case on the merits.

The free traders—led by economists like Herbert Stein of the American Enterprise Institute and Jagdish Bhagwati of Columbia University—start with the general presumption that free trade is the best economic policy for a country, whatever the rest of the world does. There is an old saw in trade theory: Saying that my country should be protectionist because other countries are is like saying that, because other countries have rocky coasts, I should block up my own harbors. They predict that any kind of confrontation with Japan will end up delivering U.S. trade policy into the hands of our own special interest groups who will wrap their selfish demands in the flag. These free traders also either discount the claims that Japan's *de jure* open markets are not open *de facto*, or adopt the legal view that internal institutional arrangements are not the business of trade law. They then argue that the United States should see to it that our own trade is as free as possible, urge other countries to do the same, and then sit back and enjoy the benefits.

The bashers, of course, view it all very differently. They see large costs to America from the asymmetry with Japan. While their gut feelings may come from conventional mercantilist sentiments, the more sophisticated bashers have learned to employ some of the modern arguments against unilateral free trade that are now current in economic theory. And the bashers therefore call for presentation of an ultimatum to Japan: Change your ways, or else!

For those in neither camp, the whole issue is agonizing. The old-time free trade position seems naive, reflecting neither the realities of Japan nor the political possibilities for America. Yet the basher program seems equally unappealing. Above all, it is virtually certain to fail in its premise: Japan will not suddenly change, and we will therefore be stuck with the "or else."

The point is that if Japan is a conspiracy, it is not a centrally directed one. There is no small group of men in Tokyo who can deliver a liberal Japanese trading regime over the course of a couple of years. Americans often find it hard to believe that Japan is a real country, with real politics, where the average member of parliament is much more concerned with pleasing his constituents (and his campaign contributors) than with keeping America mollified.

So the result of any attempt to force a radical opening of Japan's markets with the threat of U.S. protectionism will be either an embarrassing and politically costly retreat or a situation in which we must carry out our threat. Down that road lies the prospect of a fragmentation of the world into mutually protectionist trading blocs—a costly outcome though not a tragic one.

It is not easy to find a middle way. Yet in the mid-1990s it seemed as if those who were ready to be neither bashers nor apologists had been saved by the bell—because Japan suddenly looked far less threatening.

The Japanese implosion

For almost 40 years, from 1950 to 1990, the Japanese economy was consistently the most rapidly growing in the industrial world. Admittedly, the growth rate had slowed, from the torrid 9 or 10 percent annually of the 1960s to only 4 percent in the 1980s. Still, hardly anyone was prepared for what happened in the 1990s: suddenly Japanese growth stopped dead. From 1991 to 1995, the Japanese economy had almost exactly zero growth.

The detailed reasons for this growth collapse are beyond the scope of this book—and in any case are still a matter of considerable debate. The proximate cause seems to have been the bursting of a financial bubble that had driven Japanese land and stock prices to bizarre levels. The end of the "bubble economy" meant a large conventional recession, although Japan continued to have very little open unemployment. The puzzle, however, is why this recession went on and on. By 1996, although there were finally some signs of recovery, many economists had begun to wonder whether Japan's difficulties were the result of something deeper than a mere lack of demand.

At the same time, Japanese business proved itself vulnerable on other fronts. In several politically sensitive industries Japanese firms gave up some ground. In the auto industry, American manufacturers improved productivity and quality and clawed back some though not all of their lost market share. In the semiconductor industry, which many had assumed would become a Japanese province, it turned out that Japanese producers had made some crucial strategic errors: American firms continued to dominate the production of advanced chips, like the microprocessors that run personal computers, while the more mass-market chips produced in Japan were facing competition from new entrants in South Korea and elsewhere.

And the much-feared wave of Japanese direct investment in the United States turned out to have been ill-considered in many cases. The Japanese firms that had bought glamour investments like film studios soon had reason to regret their purchases; Sony, which had bought Columbia Pictures, suffered huge losses, while its rival Matsushita finally gave up and sold off its stake in MCA. Many of those Japanese investors who had bought U.S. real estate sold it back to Americans at fraction of the purchase price.

Throughout the first half of the 1990s Japan continued to run massive trade surpluses, although these were partly due to the depressed state of Japan's economy (which held down the demand for imports). And the Clinton administration at times took a hard line in trade negotiations with Japan, appearing briefly in 1994 to be on the verge of a trade war over disputes involving auto parts and other products. Nonetheless, by 1996 Americans were no longer afraid of Japan in the way they had been only a few years before, which took away much of the urgency from the Japan issue. And for those who were prepared neither to absolve Japan nor to run the risk of trade war, the travails of Japan were a cloud with a silver lining: perhaps a troubled Japan would eventually change its ways spontaneously, and the "Japan problem" would simply fade away.

IV   Financial Follies

There are certain periods in history one associates with dramatic and often disastrous wheeling and dealing on financial markets: the Roaring Twenties, the Go-Go years in the 1960s. History may never, however, have seen the kind of financial hyperactivity that has become the rule since 1980. Every year there emerge brand-new ways to speculate, while even old, well-established markets often do as much business in a day as they used to do in several months. And these hyperactive markets offer huge posibilities for reward and risk. Never in the course of human events has so much money been made—or, too often, lost—in so little time by so many people.

Why has the world of finance become so frenetic? Some people point to technology: the marriage of computers and telecommunications allows us to have both markets and market frenzies in a way that was impossible in the past. (The stock market crash of 1987 was partly due to automatic selling by computers programmed to cash out when prices fell too much—although old-fashioned human panic was the main factor.) The most important reason for the wildness of financial markets, however, is probably simply the fact that governments no longer stand in their way. Deregulation has made it possible for people to play with money in ways that used to be illegal or at least difficult.

To complete our picture of the economy, then, we look at three aspects of the financial world. First is the savings and loan affair, a classic example of how bungled deregulation can create a financial mess of startling size. Next comes a chapter that reviews some examples of vast losses in financial markets, arising from the failure of private investors to understand the new world they were living in. Finally, we turn to the turbulent but (for the United States) surprisingly peripheral events that have roiled global money markets.

12 The Savings and Loan Scandal

The conservative economic program launched by Ronald Reagan in the 1980s had two main elements. One was lower taxes; the other was deregulation—getting the government out of the private sector's way. While most economists were skeptical about the effectiveness of tax cuts for stimulating the economy, deregulation commanded wide support. Even liberal economists were persuaded by the arguments of reformers that everyone could gain from deregulation of airlines, trucking, and banking.

Yet the biggest single economic policy disaster of the 1980s sprang from a misguided attempt at deregulation. Deregulation of the savings and loan industry turned what might have been a $15 billion problem at the beginning of the decade into a $150 billion bill at the decade's end. Of course, the reasons for this debacle went deeper than simple misguided deregulatory zeal. But the rhetoric of economic freedom helped mask what might otherwise have been seen as an obviously irresponsible policy.

Origins of the crisis

Once upon a time, there was a staid, familiar institution called a savings and loan. Savings and loans were created to give ordinary people a safe way to store their money while earning modest interest. To secure the safety of this money, S&L deposits were insured by a federal agency, the Federal Savings and Loan Insurance Corporation, or FSLIC.

From the beginning, it was realized that insuring deposits created a potential source of risk and corruption. A banker whose deposits are publicly insured does not have to prove that his bank is sound. If he offers potential depositors an interest rate that is just slightly above the market rate, they will put their money in his bank, no questions asked—for they know that they cannot lose their money.

But a license to borrow as much as you like, at a fixed interest rate, is a license to gamble. Open a savings and loan; offer an interest rate a little above going rates to attract a lot of deposits; and invest the money you get in the riskiest projects you can find. If the projects work out, great—you've made a lot of money. If not, and the bank does not have enough money to repay its depositors—well, that's FSLIC's problem, not yours. It's heads you win, tails the taxpayers lose. Without the insurance, of course, your depositors would want to check on what kind of investments you were making, and if they thought you were taking too many risks, they would refuse to put money in your bank. With the insurance, they don't care.

This is an obvious problem, and until 1981 it was met with the obvious answer: eligible investments were tightly regulated and individual S&Ls were regularly audited. Lending was largely restricted to homebuyers under rules designed to prevent excessive risk taking. It was an exchange of a privilege (deposit insurance) for a responsibility (low-risk investing). And until the mid-1970s it worked quite well.

What went wrong was a risk that nobody had counted on: inflation. During the 1970s, inflation soared, and market interest rates rose along with it. At first, savings and loans simply lost depositors as the interest rates they paid grew less and less competitive with those offered by banks and money market funds. This problem was solved by allowing S&Ls to pay higher rates, but this only created a new problem. To hold their depositors, S&Ls were obliged to pay interest rates of 8, 9, or 10 percent. Meanwhile, their assets consisted of 30-year home loans made at 4, 5, or 6 percent in the days before inflation began to climb. Instead of lending out money at a higher rate than they paid on deposits, which is what banks are supposed to do, S&Ls found themselves paying more on deposits than they were earning on their assets. By 1980 many S&Ls were clearly in danger of going bankrupt.

Under the rules of the game that were supposed to be in place, this was where FSLIC was expected to do its job. Through nobody's fault, many S&Ls had made investments that in retrospect were a mistake. The solution? Shut them down, pay off their depositors, and let FSLIC cover the difference between what they had and their obligations. Estimates by economists like Robert Litan of the Brookings Institution suggest that about $15 billion in federal money would have allowed the liquidation of those S&Ls that were in real trouble, and thus ended the story.

But that's not what happened.

Double or nothing, 1981–89

The S&L story after 1980 is a simple one. Neither Congress nor the administration wanted to swallow the cost of shutting down bankrupt S&Ls. So they elected to play double or nothing: to offer the entire S&L industry a more favorable deal in return for staying in business, hoping that the problem would go away. Instead, predictably, the problem got worse.

That's not how it was portrayed at the time, of course. The ostensible purpose of the change in the rules announced in 1981 was to allow S&Ls to make more productive use of their money by substantially deregulating the investments they could make—a change justified on the general principle of free markets. But a real move to free markets would have removed the privilege of deposit insurance as the price of deregulation of investment. What the thrifts got, instead, was freedom without responsibility. They now had the right to make risky investments, while continuing to be able to assure depositors that their money was guaranteed by the federal government.

In the short run, this worked. S&Ls received a new injection of capital from high-roller entrepreneurs who were willing to maintain payments to depositors in exchange for the opportunity to gamble with their money. And S&Ls either became risk takers or were bought by people who were. All across the country savings and loans became financiers of speculative developments, projects that could conceivably make a lot of money but were more likely to lose it.

If the economy had boomed through the whole decade, if oil prices had stayed high, if real interest rates had not risen so much, it is just possible that this game of double or nothing might have worked. But, instead, oil prices collapsed, taking the price of Texas real estate with them, and the economy passed through a massive recession. Even after the recovery real interest rates remained much higher than before. By 1989 the S&Ls were in far worse shape than they had been in 1981; closing down the really troubled ones would now cost $150 billion. Even allowing for inflation, the real burden to the taxpayers was at least six times as high as it would have been had the S&L problem been dealt with at the beginning of decade.

Apportioning the blame

When the size of the S&L mess became apparent, sensational stories about the abuses of the 1980s hit the press. Tales of bank owners living high at the bank's expense, of corrupt deals, of wild risk taking made exciting reading. Yet it is not clear that the American public has absorbed the real story of what happened.

Reading the press accounts, one might imagine that what happened was some kind of mysterious invasion of immoral men— Jimmy Stewarts run out of their offices by conniving J. R. Ewings. Many of the press stories, aside from moralizing, placed the blame on the regulators for failing to keep an eye on their charges. And surely there was plenty of both corruption and malfeasance. But emphasizing these misses the point, just as focusing on the evil of the Medellín cartel misses the point of the drug problem. The great bulk of the losses came from taking bad risks, not from literal theft. And besides, Americans in general are neither better nor worse people than they used to be. So the real question has to be: What made socially destructive behavior in this industry so much more attractive than it used to be?

We already know the answer. The partial deregulation of the early 1980s made it possible for S&Ls to gamble with their depositors' money, with the federal government absorbing the risks. An S&L was worth more in the hands of a gambler than in the hands of a prudent business manager. So the owners of S&Ls either learned to be high-rollers, or were bought out by individuals who already were. Not surprisingly, the class of people who were temperamentally suited to take advantage of the opportunities offered by privilege without responsibility contained more than its share of rogues and criminals. Yet the epidemic of white-collar crime in the thrift industry was a result of the environment the government created, not an independent event.

Locking the barn door

Regulators, congressional staffers, and economists have always known the answer to the savings and loan problem: Tighten the restrictions on the S&Ls, and require the owners to put in more capital if they want to stay in business. If the capital is not forthcoming, close them down (and pay off the depositors). This was the right answer even in 1980; it is even more obviously the right answer today.

Yet this obvious answer was avoided by both the administration and Congress for nearly a decade. Even the S&L bailout scheme negotiated in 1989 was only a partial fix: It left the capital requirements on the thrifts too low and failed to allocate enough money to close down all the institutions that need to be shut. This will stretch out the problem for years to come—and quite possibly cost the taxpayers scores of billions of dollars in avoidable future payments. The whole S&L story is one of almost incredibly irresponsible federal policy, repeated year after year, and it still goes on.

Why? The U.S. government fell into two traps; it is hard to say which is the more disreputable.

First, any subsidy program, no matter how costly to the economy, creates a vested interest in its continuance. For most of the past decade there has existed a set of policies that allow shrewd operators to gamble with public funds; these operators are prepared to oppose the loss of their privileges. Given the style of the people who have come to populate the industry, they are also prepared to push their political case with a brashness and disregard for propriety that more established, genteel interest groups avoid. In the long run, the aggressiveness of the S&L industry undercuts its credibility, and threatens too many of its political allies with scandal. But the people we are talking about are not interested in the long run, and in the short run their lavishness can be effective. So the federal government has created a sort of Frankenstein monster of political economy, which may still devour many billions of dollars before it is slain.

Second, shutting the S&Ls down costs money. Worse yet, even as the foolishness of going on with double or nothing has grown, the cost of stopping the game has risen—and the restraints of federal budget cutting have grown. In the 1989 thrift plan the problem was finessed by putting the expenditures off-budget, but the trickery is straining the whole process.

What makes this sad is that paying off the depositors now is not really a cost to the taxpayers, because that cost has already been incurred. The real decision to spend taxpayer money was made long ago, when the federal government chose to encourage risk taking by institutions whose downside was publicly insured. The real cost of that decision to the economy took place when the dubious investments made by these institutions went bad; paying the depositors off now is simply giving them money they already think they have. Paying the cost of closing the S&Ls now only recognizes these costs.

There is no case for putting off the inevitable—not even concern about national saving. Even if the federal government must borrow the money with which to pay off the S&L depositors, it will not by any calculation have a negative effect on national saving. The depositors will not feel any richer—they thought they had that money anyway—so they will not increase their consumption. Meanwhile, by stopping the game, the federal government will cut its future losses. This is a clear case where the efforts of the government to avoid increasing the *measured* deficit actually aggravate the problems that deficit reduction is supposed to cure.

Is there more to come?

The S & L story is not completely over, but the main costs of cleanup have probably already been paid. The interesting and worrying question is whether the S & L story is part of a broader pattern of hidden federal liabilities.

The answer is surely yes. The S & L story is only the most extreme case of a broader phenomenon.

Start with the rest of the banking system, and in particular the commercial banks—firms like Citibank or Chase Manhattan that specialize in lending to businesses. These banks were subject to many of the same forces that led to the S & L debacle. Their profitability was eroded during the 1970s by inflation and deregulation; since they were no longer highly profitable, they were tempted to make risky loans; and the federal government encouraged them to do so by relaxing restrictions on their investment. The result was a lot of questionable lending, especially of two kinds: financing for financial schemes like leveraged buyouts, and financing for speculative real estate deals. By 1991 a number of reasonable people were warning that there might have to be a commercial bank rescue similar to the S & L bailout, with a price tag of $50–100 billion.

At the time of writing this crisis had been postponed if not necessarily avoided—but only through sheer luck. The attempts of the Federal Reserve to pull the U.S. economy out of a stubborn recession had led to very low short-term interest rates. Since these rates determine the interest rates that banks have to pay on deposits, the paradoxical result was a surge in bank profitability. Still, this windfall gain doesn't contradict the conclusion that misregulation was doing some peculiar things to bank lending during the 1980s.

There are also a number of other, fairly obscure government policies that produce hidden future liabilities. For example, there is an institution called the Pension Benefit Guarantee Corporation, which guarantees corporate pension plans in much the same way that FSLIC guaranteed thrift deposits. It turns out that there are incentives for companies to set aside insufficient money for their pension plans, then dump the problem in PBGC's lap; the federal Office of Management and Budget has estimated that there may be a hidden federal liability of $30-40 billion.

This sounds like a lot of money. Compared with the $3 trillion of additional federal debt run up during the 1980s, however, it is not that impressive. As Everett Dirksen once said about the federal budget, a billion here, a billion there, and soon you're talking about real money. The same surely applies here. If we are trying to assess the impact on our $7 trillion economy, however, it seems unlikely that any of the remaining hidden financial liabilities of the U.S. government will prove a devastating burden.

13   Losing It

On average, people with wealth to invest have done very well in the last decade. But there have also been some spectacular examples of money lost, in some cases by institutions with centuries-old reputations for probity. In this chapter we look at two such cases that happen to be both titillating and informative about the ways in which markets can go bad.

Losing it all: Lloyd's and its names[9]

It is hard to imagine making a movie about an insurance company. But the subject of the film *Lloyd's of London* is no ordinary insurance company. Founded in a coffeehouse in 1688 to insure shipping, Lloyd's was long a symbol of the British Empire. At the turn of the century it not only dominated the maritime insurance market, it accounted for half of the insurance (other than life insurance) sold in the world as a whole.

It was therefore shocking when the ancient institution began announcing multibillion-dollar losses, losses so large that the survival of Lloyd's was put in serious question. What was even more shocking, however, was the way that these institutional losses led

---

9. This account is based on "Lloyd's of London: The Failure of a Market," a case written by Robin Wells for the Stanford Business School.

to individual ruin: literally thousands of people, all of them well-to-do before they became involved with Lloyd's, had their entire personal wealth wiped out.

To understand what happened at Lloyd's, we need to understand the unusual structure of the institution, the sometimes perverse incentives created by that structure, and the reasons why that perversity has become so much more important in recent years.

Lloyd's: a peculiar market

Lloyd's is not really a corporation in the normal sense. Rather, it is a privately run market that brings together people who want to reduce their risk with other people who are willing to assume that risk for them.

The basic unit of Lloyd's is the "syndicate." A syndicate is a group of individuals, known as Names, who collectively offer insurance policies to individuals or companies who face certain kinds of risks. The original Lloyd's syndicates dealt with shipping: a merchant would go to a syndicate, and pay them a premium; if his ship was lost at sea, they would cover his losses.

Where would the money for such payments come from? To a certain extent it came from premiums themselves. For example, if a syndicate insured 100 ships, and one of them sank, the premiums from the 99 unsunk ships might be enough to pay for the losses of the sinker. But what if that turned out not to be enough? Then the personal wealth of the syndicate's members would be called upon: each member would be required to supply a fraction of the needed cash, in proportion to his stake in the syndicate.

Obviously this meant that not just anybody could become a Name—you had to prove that you had the kind of financial resources that would let you fulfill your obligations if necessary. If you could offer such proof, however, you could then enter into an unusual but traditionally very profitable business arrangement. On becoming a Name, you did not have to invest any money (actually you had to put up some cash, but this was a fairly minor detail). All you had to do was pledge to meet a certain share of the syndicate's losses if necessary, and you were then entitled to the same share of the syndicate's profits. If the syndicate was profitable, as most syndicates historically have been, you would basically receive money for nothing. And so being allowed to become a Name has traditionally been regarded as a rare privilege, a sort of lucrative honor bestowed on the right sort of person.

Suppose, however, that a syndicate did lose money. How much could you, as a Name, lose in the process? The answer was . . . everything. By ancient tradition, Lloyd's operates on the basis of unlimited personal liability. That is, a Name is not like a stockholder in a corporation, who can at most lose the money he has invested. If a syndicate loses enough money—that is, if it finds itself obliged to pay out sufficiently large claims—then the Names who belong to that syndicate may be required to strip themselves of everything they own, right down to their homes. And in the 1990s that is just what happened to large numbers of respectable people—businessmen, widows, members of the aristocracy, and, to the great embarrassment of the British government, several members of Parliament. A few of these ruined individuals committed suicide; the rest began a series of bitter legal actions against the management.

How could this happen? To a certain extent the Lloyd's crisis, like the savings and loan crisis we looked at in chapter 12, was the result of bad luck: the late 1980s and early 1990s were marked by an unusual number of natural disasters and other problems—notably massive lawsuits against the manufacturers of asbestos insulation. But just as fortune favors the prepared, bad luck most hurts those who court it. The fundamental source of the Lloyd's debacle was that the institution's whole structure created incentives to take bad risks.

Managers versus Names

The key thing to understand about Lloyd's is that the "managing agencies" that ran syndicates did not necessarily share the interests of the Names they represented—even though these managers were normally Names themselves. There were at least two ways in which a managing agent might have strongly different priorities from those of the Names for whom he worked. First, management collected fees for writing insurance; this created an incentive to insure lots of dubious risks for the fees, leaving the Names to face the costs if the risks went bad. Second, more subtly but perhaps even more seriously, each management agency typically ran several syndicates in closely related areas. This created an incentive for unscrupulous managers to play favorites—steering the good risks to syndicates in which they themselves were Names, and the bad risks to syndicates in which they were not.

The potential for misbehavior was greatly increased by the new opportunities for risk-taking created by an increasingly complex insurance market. By the 1980s the traditional Lloyd's role as insurer of ships and their cargoes was long gone. Indeed, Lloyd's for the most part did not offer insurance policies directly to the public. Instead, it focused on the activity known as "reinsurance." In this activity, the original seller of insurance tries to limit its own risk by itself buying insurance against heavy losses. For example, an insurance company that has insured houses in some area may take out an insurance policy of its own that protects it against having to pay out more than $10 million. Whoever offers the reinsurance takes on a large but low-probability risk: it is unlikely that so many homes in that area will be destroyed at the same time, but if they are—say by a hurricane—the reinsurer will abruptly have to make a large payment. And as it happens there were some unexpectely destructive hurricanes in the late 1980s and early 1990s; Lloyd's syndicates bore a disproportionate share of the resulting losses.

There is, of course, nothing wrong with taking risks, as long as you know what you are doing. Many Names, however, probably did not understand how risky it was to become mainly reinsurers rather than original sellers. Moreover, the potential for exploitation of unwary Names was increased further with the introduction of so-called London Market Excess (LMX) reinsurance. This was re-reinsurance: a reinsurer who had agreed to pay all claims in excess of, say $10 million would in turn buy a policy insuring against losses of more than $50 million. Such LMX policies were, of course, even more risky to offer than ordinary reinsurance: if they kicked in, huge sums would have to be supplied. Moreover, they created an opportunity for managers to pad their fees. A manager who ran several syndicates could write a reinsurance policy at one of the syndicates he controlled, collecting a fee there; then reinsure that policy at a second such syndicate, collecting another fee; then take out yet a third policy, and so on. The process came to be known as "making a turn," and it sometimes reached ludicrous proportions: when an oil rig blew up in 1988 with an actual loss of $1.4 billion, the payments of insurance, reinsurance, re-re-insurance, and so on were more than 10 times as large.

Of course, Lloyd's had some rules that were supposed to prevent Names from getting in over their heads. The key rule was the "premium income limit," which said that the premiums from all the syndicates in which a Name was involved could not exceed a certain fraction of the Name's wealth. The problem was that this rule became ineffective once syndicates began concentrating on unlikely but severe catastrophes. Oil rigs do not explode often, so the premium for insuring such a rig will not be large; but if it does explode, the costs to the insuring syndicate will be huge, and can wipe out its members.

Does all this sound familiar? It should: the problems at Lloyd's involved "moral hazard," and bore a strong family resemblance to those at the savings and loans we looked at in Chapter 12. There too managers had an incentive to take excessive risks, to gamble with other peoples' money; Lloyd's reinsured oil rigs while S&Ls financed shopping malls, but the basic principle was the same.

In the case of the savings and loans the opportunity for sharp practice arose because the federal government guaranteed deposits, so that depositors had no reason to monitor what their banks were up to. Names had no such guarantee. Why didn't they ride herd on their managers?

The answer was that Lloyd's, over the course of its long and illustrious history, had taken care to cultivate a reputation for probity. Over the centuries, Names had always been able to trust Lloyd's managers to act responsibly, precisely because they knew how concerned the institution was about preserving that reputation. It never occurred to them that times had changed.

But why had they changed?

The decline of Lloyd's

In its prime, the way Lloyd's was run offered a strong defense against moral hazard, based on the concern of both the institution as a whole and the managers of individual syndicates for reputation.

Until the 1960s, only those who worked at Lloyd's in some capacity—as managers, underwriters, or brokers—were allowed to become Names. This had the direct consequence of ensuring that Names were pretty well informed both about the business in general and about the reputations of syndicate managers. It also meant that managers and their Names were involved in a lot of reciprocal dealing over long periods of time: if a manager abused the trust of his Names one year, he would not be invited to be a Name when they or their friends opened a syndicate the next.

Adding to the effectiveness of this social sanction was the profitability of Lloyd's. For most of its history, the unique position of Lloyd's meant that being associated with it really was a lucrative privilege. To be a manager or underwriter, and to be allowed to be a Name, was to be part of an exclusive club whose members were more or less guaranteed both social cachet and a comfortable income. Few would risk losing that position for the sake of a temporary increase in fees. In this sense those who worked at Lloyd's were just like banks in the good old days, highly rewarded because they were protected from competition, cautious in their actions because they did not want to kill a goose that kept on laying golden eggs. The profitability of Lloyd's was the result of a special market position rather than government regulation, but it had the same effect.

What eventually went wrong was, of course, that the world changed. Conventional insurance companies crowded into lines of business that Lloyd's had once had to itself, and were often more efficient because they did not have Lloyd's archaic management methods. For a time Lloyd's was able to retain its role simply because of the advantages that came from sheer scale; but eventually corporate competitors began to rival Lloyd's in that dimension too. Little by little, the value of being a member of the club declined—and so therefore did the incentive to retain a good reputation.

As in the case of the savings and loans, the growing problem was met by a change in regulations that seemed to offer a way out but in the end made things much worse—with the difference, again, being that these were not government regulations but internal rules. In the 1960s, in an effort to make Lloyd's more competitive by making it bigger, the institution was thrown open to Names who were not involved in the business—"external Names" as opposed to the "working Names" who had previously been the only sources of capital. By the 1990s less than one-fifth of Lloyd's Names worked there. The result was a large influx of money into Lloyd's, and a resulting expansion of its business— but also a deterioration in both the knowledgeability of the typical Name and the incentive of managers to serve their Names well. And so the stage was set for catastrophe.

The Lloyd's story repeats some of the lessons of the savings and loan affair. It also illustrates a point that we can sometimes forget in the 1990s, when faith in the powers of free markets has become axiomatic among many people: While government mis-regulation can screw up a market, it is not necessary. Sometimes the private sector can mess things up all by itself.

To reinforce that point, let us turn to another example of finan-cial follies: the strange story of how one company created chaos in the world copper market.

How copper came a cropper

In early 1995 the world was astonished to hear that a young employee of the 138-year-old British firm Barings had lost more than a billion dollars in speculative trading, quite literally break-ing the bank. It turned out that an inexperienced 28-year-old trad-er named Nick Leeson, based in Singapore, had been engaged in massive speculation in Japanese stock market futures (promises to buy or sell stocks at a later date)—apparently without any effec-tive supervision from his superiors. He bought large numbers of such futures in the hope that the market would go up. When it went down instead, he bought even more, like a gambler trying to win back his losses. Eventually, when the losses reached more than $1.24 billion, he fled the country, eventually to be appre-hended in Germany. A series of similar if less spectacular events were meanwhile occurring at other firms; the term "rogue trader" entered the language, meaning an employee who uses the complexity of modern financial markets to gamble with his employer's money.

People quickly become blasé. When an even bigger financial disaster was revealed in the summer of 1996—the loss of at least $1.8 billion (the true number is rumored to be $4 billion or more) in the copper market by an employee of Sumitomo Metals—the story quickly faded from the front pages. "Oh well, just another rogue trader," was the general reaction.

It soon became clear, however, that Yasuo Hamanaka was not, like Nick Leeson of Barings, a poorly supervised employee using his company's money to gamble on unpredictable markets. On the contrary, he was in fact doing something much more interesting: implementing a deliberate corporate strategy of "cornering" the world copper market—a strategy that initially worked, yielding large profits. Hubris brought him down in the end; but it is his initial success, not his eventual failure, that is the informative part of the tale.

How to corner a market

To understand what Sumitomo was up to, you don't need to know many details about the copper market. The essential facts about copper (and many other commodities) are that (i) it is subject to wide fluctuations in the balance between supply and demand, and (ii) it can be stored, so that production need not be consumed at once. These two facts mean that a certain amount of speculation is a normal and necessary part of the way the market works: it is inevitable and desirable that people should try to buy low and sell high, building up inventories when the price is perceived to be unusually low and running those inventories down when the price seems to be especially high.

So far so good. But a long time ago somebody—I wouldn't be surprised if it was a Phoenician tin merchant in the first millenium B.C.—realized that a clever man with sufficiently deep pockets could basically hold up such a market for ransom. The details are often mind-numbingly complex, but the principle is simple. Buy up a large part of the supply of whatever commodity you are trying to corner—it doesn't really matter whether you actually take claim to the stuff itself or buy up "futures," which are nothing but promises to deliver the stuff on a specified date—then deliberately keep some but not all of what you have bought off the market, to sell later. What you have now done, if you have pulled it off, is created an artificial shortage that sends prices soaring, allowing you to make big profits on the stuff you do sell. You may be obliged to take some loss on the supplies you have withheld from the market, selling them later at lower prices, but if you do it right this loss will be far smaller than your gain from higher current prices.

This may sound a bit like a magic trick. Why does it work? Think for a moment of the market for copper as spanning only two periods, Now and Later. And suppose that you have already locked up a large part of the supply of copper that will become available Now. When you withhold some of those supplies from the market, you are in effect "shipping" them from one market— the market for copper Now—to the other market, that for copper Later.

This shipment will presumably not be profitable in its own right. That is, either the price Later will be lower than the price Now, or at any rate will not be sufficiently higher to cover the costs of storing the metal, including the interest cost on the money tied up in the process. (Why do we know this? Because if storing metal for the future was profitable, somebody else would already be doing it.) So withholding copper from the market means losing at least some money on the copper held back.

What makes this "shipment" worth doing, however, is its effect on prices. By holding copper off the market Now and selling it Later, you drive prices up Now and down Later. But you already own a lot of the copper that will be sold Now, so the higher price will raise your profits. On the other hand, you do not own a comparable amount of the copper that will be sold Later, so the lower price then will not produce an offsetting loss. In short, even if you actually lose money on the copper you hold off the market, you may more than make it up by raising the price at which you can sell the rest.

Of course, the more copper you hold off the market, the less you are trying to sell Now and the more you are trying to sell Later. So there are limits to how far you can push this game—or to be more precise, there is an optimal amount of copper to ship to the future, which is positive but not too large. Still, there is no question that it is often possible to make a lot of money if you can succeed in temporarily cornering a market.

Sumitomo's success

Cornering a market is nice work if you can get it; but you must surmount several serious hurdles. First, you must be able to operate on a sufficiently large scale—you must be able to buy enough of the supply both to move the price up and profit when it does so. Second, the strategy only works if not too many people realize what you are up to when you are buying up the supply—otherwise they will anticipate the run-up in prices and refuse to sell to you in the first place unless you offer a price so high that the game no longer pays. Third, this kind of thing is, for obvious reasons, quite illegal. (The first Phoenician who tried it probably got very rich; the second got sacrificed to Moloch.)

The amazing thing is that Sumitomo managed to overcome all of these obstacles. The world copper market is immense; nonetheless, a single trader apparently was able and willing to dominate that market. In the modern information age, you might have thought that the kind of secrecy required for such a massive market manipulation was impossible—but Hamanaka pulled it off, partly by working through British intermediaries, but mainly through a covert alliance with Chinese firms (some of them state-owned). And as for the regulators . . . well, what about the regulators?

In a way, that is the most puzzling part of the Sumitomo story. If Hamanaka had really been nothing more than an employee run wild, one could not really fault regulators for failing to rein him in; that would have been his employer's job. But he wasn't; he was, in effect, engaged in a price-fixing conspiracy on his employer's behalf. And while it may not have been obvious what Sumitomo was up to when it started, the role of "Mr. Copper" and his company in manipulating prices has apparently been common knowledge for years among anyone familiar with the copper market. Why was he allowed to continue?

The answer may in part be that the global nature of his activities made it unclear who had responsibility. Should it have been Japan, because Sumitomo is headquarted there? Should it have been Britain, home of the London Metal Exchange? Should it have been the United States, where much of the copper Sumitomo ended up owning is warehoused? Beyond this confusion over responsibility, however, one suspects that regulators were inhibited by the uncritically pro-market ideology of our times. Many people nowadays take it as an article of faith that free markets always take care of themselves—that there is no need to regulate people like Hamanaka, because the market will automatically punish their presumption.

Sumitomo's failure

Sumitomo's strategy did indeed eventually come to grief—but only because Hamanaka apparently could not bring himself to face the fact that even the most successful market manipulator must accept an occasional down along with the ups. In particular, remember our analysis of a market corner: you will normally lose money on the copper (or other commodity) you keep off the market, making it up with the higher price at which you sell the rest. Hamanaka, however, seems to have forgotten the logic of his own strategy. Rather than sell some of his copper at a loss, he chose to play double or nothing, trying to repeat his initial success by driving prices ever higher, hoping eventually to unload it on unsuspecting buyers. Since a market corner is necessarily a sometime thing, his unwillingness to let go led to disaster. But had he been a bit more flexible and realistic, Sumitomo could have walked away from the copper market with modest losses offset by enormous, ill-gotten gains.

The funny thing about the Sumitomo affair is that if you ignore the exotic trimmings—the Japanese names, the Chinese connection—it's a story right out of the robber baron era, when freebooting capitalists like Jay Gould and Jim Fisk routinely manipulated markets and looted the savings of the unwary. The story of the savings and loan disaster might make it seem as if bad things happen to markets only when government regulators create perverse incentives. The Sumitomo affair, like the story of Lloyd's, is a reminder that markets can go bad even when the government stays out—and reminds us why government regulators were brought in in the first place.

14 Global Finance

One of the surprising things about the big financial events in the United States during the 1980s—the savings and loan debacle, the rise and fall of the junk bond market, and such less heralded events as the emergence of huge markets in strange new assets like mortgage-backed securities—was how relentlessly domestic they were. A savings and loan association is a quintessentially American institution, and the scandal was largely played out in the small cities and towns of the American heartland. The wave of leveraged buyouts was largely confined to the United States. Foreign firms increased their stake in the U.S. economy, but they did so largely through friendly acquisitions, not the hostile takeovers favored by our own corporate raiders; and these raiders rarely made forays overseas. The financial excitement of the 1980s was a homegrown affair.

Why was this surprising? Because the word "global" has become a favorite buzzword for commentators on economic affairs. Indeed, it has become almost pro forma for businesspeople to talk in hushed tones about the extraordinary international mobility of capital, which supposedly integrates the world into a seamless whole. Walter Wriston, the former chairman of Citibank, expressed this new conventional wisdom in a 1992 book entitled

The Twilight of Sovereignty: How Information Technology is Changing the World, in which he argued that computers and telecommunications, by linking national markets, were making national policymakers increasingly ineffectual.

Much of this is hype. International financial events have been surprisingly peripheral to U.S. economic affairs since 1980. It is hard to think of any shock originating outside the United States since the 1979 surge in oil prices that has had a really major impact on the U.S. economy, and even that had little to do with financial markets. Yet while global financial markets have not had a major impact on actual events, they have fascinated many influential people—and that is in itself a reason to review some of the main features of these markets.

How global is the global market?

On any given day, huge sums of money are moved around the world. Surveys show that during 1989 world foreign exchange transactions, in which individuals and firms convert their funds from one currency into another, exceeded $500 billion every *day*. The vast bulk of these transactions involved purchases of assets rather than goods and services; that is, there were massive international movements of capital.

Nonetheless, in spite of this frenetic pace of business, it would be premature to conclude that national boundaries have become irrelevant. Indeed, in some ways the links between national capital markets are surprisingly weak.

For one thing, while there is a lot of trading, relatively few investors seem willing to make long-term commitments to foreign markets. There is remarkably little international diversification of portfolios—that is, Americans are rarely stockholders of foreign companies, and conversely. Estimates suggest that more than 90 percent of the value of stocks owned by American residents is still in American companies; the same is true of Japanese and European investors.[10]

Perhaps because there is so little international "cross-holding" of stocks, world stock markets do not necessarily move together. This was illustrated spectacularly from 1990 to 1992, when the Japanese stock market—which at its peak was worth more than the U.S. market—began a prolonged slide. Over the course of two years, the Nikkei index fell more than 60 percent. In a closely integrated capital market, one might have thought that such a huge decline in what was at the beginning the world's biggest market would drag down other markets as well. Yet in fact stock prices in the United States and Europe actually rose over the same period.

Finally, there is surprisingly limited long-term capital movement, even when compared with past experience. Japan saved 18 percent of its income in the 1980s, twice the average of other advanced nations. One might have expected the Japanese to invest a large share of those savings abroad. In fact, the average capital outflow was only 2 percent of national income, about 11 percent of total savings. By contrast, the United Kingdom invested 40 percent of its savings abroad over the 40-year period ending in 1913. By this measure, at least, we seem to have a less effective global capital market in the age of computers than we did in the age of steam.

Although the global capital market is less global than we sometimes tend to imagine, it is not totally unimportant. So let's turn to several cases in which international financial events were thought to be crucial by U.S. policymakers.

---

10. Compare this with the situation within the United States: California residents show virtually no preference for owning the stocks of California-based as opposed to, say, New York-based companies.

Third World debt

During the 1970s, private bankers in the United States and else-where decided that lending to Third World countries was a good idea. Loans to governments, or loans guaranteed by govern-ments, looked safe enough to the bankers to make the higher yields on Third World lending attractive—as Citibank's Walter Wriston asserted, in remarks he was later to regret, "Sovereign nations don't go bankrupt."

As long as the flow of money continued, everything looked fine: The debtor countries could pay interest and principal easily out of the new loans. In 1981 and 1982, however, for a variety of reasons, confidence evaporated, and the flow of money dried up with it—and it turned out that the countries could not generate enough cash to service their debt. The result was a rolling crisis that continued through the rest of the decade.

Third World debt figures prominently in many pictures of the world economy in the 1980s. In human terms this is clearly appropriate. Most of Latin America and most of Sub-Saharan Africa, as well as a few other nations like the Philippines, were hard hit by the debt crisis. Economic growth in the highly indebt-ed countries (HICs) was far slower after 1981 than before. Unemployment and inflation soared, living standards of already very poor families deteriorated. For some of those at the bottom in Latin America (and even more so in Africa), the debt crisis was lethal.

As a concern of U.S. *economic* policy, however, the debt crisis was not a major issue. The unfortunate fact about poor countries is that they don't have much money—and so, in purely economic terms, they do not carry much weight. The combined gross national products of all troubled debtors were less than 4 percent of the world's GNP. The total value of all loans to troubled debtors was less than 1 percent of the wealth of the creditor nations; the debt service on those loans less than one-quarter of 1 percent of the national incomes of the creditors. Terrible as it is to say, the United States did not have a strong economic interest in what happens to Third World debtors.

Nonetheless, for much of the 1980s the problems of Third World debtor countries were a subject of high-level policy concern, for two main reasons.

First, in the early years of the debt crisis there was a fear that defaults by debtor countries could help trigger a banking crisis. Although the sums of money involved were not large compared with the world economy as a whole, claims on troubled debtors were concentrated in the hands of the largest banks; since the onset of the debt crisis coincided with a severe recession in the United States and Europe, policymakers worried that losses in the Third World could tip crucial "money center" banks over the edge. This danger receded as the Western economies recovered; by the late 1980s, bank regulators were much more worried about bad loans to real estate developers than they were about outstanding claims on Brazil or Mexico.

Second, the creditor nations felt that they had an interest in preserving the political stability of debtors, and they feared that a confrontation between debtors and bankers could lead to radicalization. In 1982 the picture of an anti-American movement rising to power in Mexico by denouncing foreign banks and demanding debt repudiation did not seem farfetched. Indeed, it could still happen — not this year or next, but it would be foolish to imagine that resentment of rich nations has vanished from the world.

So officials at the Federal Reserve, the U.S. Treasury, and the International Monetary Fund believed that they had to take a hand in the debt problem. But what was the right policy?

Financing vs. forgiving

Suppose that someone who owes you money approaches you and tells you that he cannot pay in full. After checking out the story, you find that he is telling the truth, and that no purpose would be served by trying to force him to come up with the money. What do you do? You have two basic choices. You can give him time by postponing the payment, in effect lending him the money he cannot pay, and hope that he will be able to pay later. Or you can tell him to pay what he can, and consider the account settled (except that you probably will not lend him money again for a long time). The same basic options confronted the creditors of the Third World: They could either *finance* the debt—that is, postpone the countries' obligations and hope that things will look better later on—or they could *forgive* it, reduce the debtors' obligations to a level that they may be able to pay.

From 1982 until 1989, official policy toward Third World debt was based on the premise that financing was enough, that if debtor nations were given time, they would eventually be able to meet their obligations. Then, in March 1989, Treasury Secretary Nicholas Brady declared that the United States was now advocating a strategy of debt reduction.

During the years of the financing strategy, the obligations of countries were postponed in three ways. Repayment of principal was rescheduled; official agencies such as the IMF and the World Bank made new loans to the countries that could be used to pay part of the interest coming due; and the banks that had lent money to the countries in the first place were rounded up for so-called "concerted" lending, which amounted to indirect relending of part of the remaining interest. In effect, repayment of debt was very nearly halted, and limited new lending was arranged from both private and public sources.

This strategy could be, and was, described as a plan to put highly indebted countries still deeper into debt. In the early years of the debt problem, however, this did not seem like a bad idea. Given the rates of growth achieved by debtor nations in the past, and the economic reforms insisted on by the creditors as part of the package, it seemed likely that most of the major debtors could grow their way out of their debt problem. In other words, even though the debt might grow, the incomes of the debtors would grow faster—and thus the creditworthiness of the debtors would improve, not worsen, over time.

By 1989, however, nearly everyone agreed that this strategy had failed. The main problem was that growth in the most heavily indebted countries had simply failed to live up to expectations. The major debtor nations had managed growth rates of 5 percent or more in the years before the crisis. After 1982 they hardly grew at all, which meant that their per capita income fell steadily as their populations increased. It remains uncertain how much of the slowdown was due to the debt crisis itself, but the result was clear: political demands for debt reduction grew within the debtor countries, while the lack of growth discouraged potential investors. The prospect of regaining access to world financial markets seemed more remote than ever: in early 1989 the secondary market price of Third World debt—the price at which creditors sell claims to each other—averaged only 30 percent of face value.

As a result, in 1989 Nicholas Brady, the Secretary of the Treasury, announced U.S. support for a strategy of reducing Third World debt. Within six months Mexico had negotiated a "Brady deal" to reduce its debt; over the next three years most other major debtors followed suit.

And then something strange happened.

The "emerging markets" phenomenon

The debt reductions involved in the Brady deals were not very large. For example, Mexico managed to reduce its debt by only about 10 percent—hardly enough, one might think, to make a big difference to its economic situation. And yet almost as soon as the deal was signed, there was a transformation in that situation. It was as if debt reduction, however small, was a signal to the financial markets to reassess the debtor countries. And suddenly Third World countries, under the new name of "emerging markets," were regarded as attractive places to invest. By 1993 Mexico and Argentina were attracting capital at a faster rate than they had in the 1970s.

The new flows of capital to developing countries took different forms from the previous wave. There is virtually no new lending from banks. Instead, there was a mixture of direct foreign investment by multinational corporations; large-scale investment in "emerging" stock markets; and purchases of private bonds, often brokered by the same firms that sold domestic junk bonds in the United States during the 1980s.

Mexico provides the clearest case. Foreign firms, such as U.S. auto companies, have been building factories in Mexico to produce for the U.S. market. Investors have been buying Mexican stocks—the Mexican stock market rose more than 400 percent in dollar terms between the end of 1988 and the end of 1991. And private Mexican investors, like the group of entrepreneurs building a toll road to service the booming northern region, have been selling bonds abroad. Overall capital inflows, negligible between 1982 and 1989, were more than 8 percent of GDP in 1993.

Why did market sentiment change so rapidly? Part of the answer is that Brady deals satisfied the political need to take a pound of flesh out of creditors, freeing countries to move ahead. Another part of the answer is that some debtor nations put their own houses in order, balancing budgets, reducing inflation, freeing up their trade and selling off government-owned companies. But capital started to flow even to countries like Brazil, which has yet to bring its budget or inflation rate under control, let alone put together a serious long-term reform plan.

It's hard to escape the suspicion that there was a strong psychological element to the change of opinion.

The tequila effect

During the course of 1994 Mexico began to experience some troubling difficulties. Some of them were political. The world was startled when at the beginning of the year peasants in the poor, backward state of Chiapas launched an armed uprising. The uprising posed no real threat to government authority, but it revealed a depth of discontent that few had appreciated. Later in the year the presidential candidate of the ruling Institutional Revolutionary Party was mysteriously assassinated; though a replacement (a mild-mannered, U.S.-educated economist) was quickly found and duly elected, the assassination reinforced the sense that things were not fully under control. Meanwhile, the economy was not doing as well as expected: growth had slowed, unemployment was rising, and reserves of foreign currency were declining.

A few economists inside Mexico and a larger number outside argued that owing to inflation which, though slowing, had outpaced inflation in the United States, the Mexican peso had become overvalued. Mexican industry, they argued, had become uncompetitive with industry elsewhere; and they urged that this situation be corrected with a devaluation of the peso. Mexican officials demurred, partly out of the belief that such a devaluation would lose the country the confidence of investors, partly because they did not want to take such a step before the election. In December 1994, however, after the election had been won, a devaluation actually took place.

It turned out to be a disaster—although it remains unclear whether it was the idea or the implementation that was at fault.

The initial devaluation was smaller than most people thought necessary, so it was taken by investors not as a finished event but as a "first bite of the cherry," a sign of further devaluation to come. Worse, news of the plan had been leaked to Mexican insiders in advance, reinforcing foreign investors' suspicion that they could not trust Mexico; and the new finance minister quickly alienated these same investors with his perceived arrogance. In a short time the peso had crashed to half its former value. Moreover, this loss of confidence spread to other emerging market nations, such as Argentina—the so-called "tequila effect."

During 1995 Mexico was able to stabilize the peso through a combination of high interest rates and a large temporary loan arranged by the United States. Argentina, which had committed itself to a fixed exchange rate of one peso per dollar, was able to defend that rate with its own high-interest-rate policy and a smaller loan from the World Bank. But this financial stabilization came at a high cost: both countries plunged into recession, with Mexico experiencing a stunning 7 percent decline in output. By 1996 a fairly strong recovery appeared to be under way in Mexico, and a shakier one in Argentina (which had not suffered as deep an initial slump). Still, the whole experience was troubling.

It was not hard to explain why the overheated enthusiasm of investors for Mexico and Argentina had cooled somewhat. Both countries had real economic weaknesses, which many economists had pointed out to little avail during the years of euphoria. Still, these weaknesses were not sufficient to explain the sheer extent of the crisis. As World Bank economist Guillermo Calvo put it, the mystery was why the punishment had been so much greater than the crime.

The best answer seemed to be that the loss of investor confidence precipitated a sort of self-fulfilling political/economic cycle of crisis. What worried investors was not so much the fundamental economic situation as concerns that the political consensus for free-market oriented reforms would fail. Because they were nervous about the political situation, investors were unwilling to keep money in those countries unless compensated by very high interest rates. The biggest threat to the politics of reform came, however, from the depressed state of the economies—which were depressed precisely because of the need to keep interest rates so high! In effect, investors were saying, "I won't keep my money in Mexico because I am worried about the stability of the political system; what endangers that system is the depression caused by the need to keep interest rates high to satisfy worried investors like me." This may sound irrational, and from the point of view of the collective interest of the investors, it was. From the point of view of any one investor, however, it made perfect sense.

Whatever the eventual outcome of the financial crisis in emerging markets, the whole story had some disturbing implications. If the analysis of the crisis given above is correct, many countries may be vulnerable to what amount to the whims of the capital markets. A country need not follow unsound policies to get in trouble; all that need happen is for investors to conclude, for whatever reason, that the country is at risk—and their loss of confidence will produce a crisis that justifies their fears.

The G7 and policy coordination

In 1985, at a famous meeting at the Plaza Hotel, finance ministers from the five largest industrial economies met to try to push down the value of the dollar. Somewhat to their own surprise, they succeeded; and as a result consultations between major industrial countries to discuss and in principle coordinate their financial policies became a regular event. The original group of five was extended to include Italy and Canada, creating the Group of Seven, or G7. The G7 now holds annual summits and more frequent meetings of finance ministers.

G7 meetings are lavish affairs that provide excellent photo opportunities, and calls for effective international coordination are a favorite topic for economics writers who want to sound sophisticated and forward-looking. There is at least one well-funded private organization, the G7 Council, that holds conferences simply to discuss G7 affairs. But are G7 meetings—or as afficionados like to call them, the "G7 process"—really important to the United States?

The answer, surprisingly, is probably not.

The economics of interdependence

It sounds on the face of it like a good idea for advanced countries to coordinate their macroeconomic policies. After all, who wants uncoordinated policies? But what, specifically, are the benefits of coordination?

There is a standard argument for coordination, which may be illustrated by the following story: suppose that the industrial world as a whole is in a recession. Now suppose that an individual country wants to increase domestic demand in order to get out of the recession. It can do this either by cutting interest rates, to stimulate private investment, or by providing a fiscal stimulus (a tax cut or a public spending increase). But if it moves unilaterally, either policy may get it into trouble. If it tries to expand by cutting interest rates, investors will try to move their money elsewhere in search of higher yields, driving down the value of the country's currency—and this may be inflationary. If it tries to expand using fiscal policy, part of the expansion of demand will fall on imports, leading to a growing trade deficit. So a country may be unwilling to embark on a unilateral policy of trying to end a recession.

But suppose that the major nations can agree to a joint, coordinated expansion. Then the picture is different. If they all cut interest rates together, investors will stay put and nobody's currency will need to fall. Alternatively, if they all engage in fiscal expansion together, each country will see its exports as well as its imports go up, so that trade deficits need not rise, and each country's growth will be reinforced by the stimulus from these higher exports. So the countries may be able to do collectively what none of them is willing to do alone. In principle, then, by agreeing to coordinate their policies, countries can be more effective in dealing with global recessions.

So there is a solid conceptual basis for the idea of international policy coordination. There's only one problem: it just isn't very important in practice, because international trade is of only limited importance to the world's large economies.

The limited importance of coordination

You can get a sense of the limited importance of the G7 process by considering the economic relationships between the United States and the European Union. In absolute terms the two economies do a huge amount of trade. In 1995 the United States exported $85 billion to the EU, and imported approximately the same amount. But these are huge economies, and the trade between them is a surprisingly small fraction of their output: U.S. exports to the EU are less than 2 percent of our GDP.

Now suppose that the EU were to engage in a huge program of spending increases and tax cuts that led to a 10 percent expansion in the EU economy. What would this do for the U.S. economy?

When an economy recovers from a recession, its imports usually grow more rapidly than its output; the historical ratio is about two to one. So a 10 percent expansion of the EU economy might mean a 20 percent rise in U.S. exports to the EU, which sounds impressive. But since the initial level of exports to the EU is only 2 percent of our GDP, the overall expansionary impact would be only 0.4 percent of GDP—significant, but not of overwhelming importance.

This example involves an expansion program far larger than is ever likely to be negotiated in a G7 meeting. In 1993 Japan agreed to a stimulus package of record size, and even this was expected to raise Japan's GDP by less than 3 percent. Furthermore, Japan would probably have done most of the expansion even without pressure from its G7 partners. The G7 process probably led to a slightly larger Japanese stimulus than would otherwise have happened, and this in turn probably helped expand the U.S. and European economies a little faster than would otherwise have been the case, but it is hard to believe that the net impact on the U.S. economy was more than 0.1 percent of GDP.

The idea of economic policy coordination has attracted a huge amount of economic research over the past decade. There are strong incentives to find reasons why policy coordination is important: it's a glamorous subject, you get to go to fancy meetings, and high officials very much want to hear how much they matter. The conclusion of most studies has, however, been negative. There just isn't much payoff to getting together to set common monetary and fiscal policies.

Does it do any harm?

Even if G7 meetings don't accomplish much, can't they be regarded as a relatively harmless way for officials to spend their time?[11]

Certainly on the scale of things that officials do, international meetings to discuss policy coordination are fairly benign. There are only two risks. The first is simply one of distraction: officials may pay too much attention to glamorous-sounding but unimportant international issues while neglecting domestic priorities. (The United States would have been better off if top officials had

11. In 1992 the *Wall Street Journal* ran a very funny pseudo-anthropological report on Multilateral Man, the species who attends international conferences such as G7 meetings. They described him as believing in two propositions: we must cooperate to improve coordination, and coordinate to improve cooperation.

paid less attention during the 1980s to Third World debt and more to what has happening to boring domestic savings and loan associations.)

The other risk is that when countries fail to do much to help each other, as they usually will, they will start blaming each other instead. Japan cannot pull the United States out of a recession, or vice versa—but it's not clear that senior officials always understand that, and unrealistic expectations about the benefits from coordination could turn into a new source of international tension.

Europe's monetary woes

International policy coordination is not an important issue for the United States, because there isn't enough interdependence among the big economies to make it one. But this does not mean that international monetary issues are never important. In fact, the early 1990s were marked by a spectacular international monetary drama played out within Europe. The United States was not an active participant in this drama, and it had few direct repercussions for our own economy. Nonetheless, it was such a major part of world events that it seems worth describing briefly.

Why Europe is different

International policy coordination among the big players—the United States, the European Union as a whole, and Japan—is not very important. Within Europe, however, the interdependence of national economic policies has been crucial to understanding events in recent years.

One reason is simply that because Europe is such a compact area, its nations do much more trade with each other than they do with countries on other continents. France's exports to the United States are less than 2 percent of its GDP; its exports to other

European Union countries are 15 percent of GDP. Thus the French economy is much more strongly affected by the economic policies of its neighboring countries than by the policies of Japan or the United States. The rationale for coordination described earlier is much more important within Europe than for the global economy as a whole.

In the 1980s this natural interdependence was greatly reinforced by the decision of all major European countries to link their monetary policies in the European Monetary System.

The European Monetary System or EMS was founded in 1979. Its initial purpose was to limit the fluctuations of exchange rates within Europe, fluctuations that had allegedly been creating unnecessary uncertainty for business.[12] On paper, it was simply an agreement to stabilize exchange rates within a set of agreed ranges. For example, in 1992 there was a "central parity" of 3.36 French francs per German mark; if the actual exchange rate went either above or below that rate by 2.25 percent, France and Germany were supposed to buy or sell each others' currencies to keep it from going any further. Countries cannot change their central parities unilaterally: they must meet and agree with the other members of the system on a new set of parities.

In practice, the EMS was much more than an exchange rate arrangement. It is not possible for a government to stabilize an exchange rate for very long simply by intervening on the foreign exchange market. Suppose that a country tries simultaneously to have an expansionary domestic monetary policy and support the value of its currency. By reducing domestic interest rates it will provide investors with an incentive to move money out of the country. If it then tries to support its currency by buying it on the foreign exchange market, it is trying to undo with its left hand

---

12. There is a technical difference between the EMS, which is the overall treaty, and the Exchange Rate Mechanism or ERM that obliges countries to stabilize their currencies. At the time of writing, the United Kingdom remains a member of the EMS but not of the ERM. This legalistic point will be ignored in the text.

what it is doing with its right. In practice, a commitment to stabilize the exchange rate must be backed by the willingness to raise interest rates to defend the currency.

So the EMS in effect linked the monetary policies of European countries together. But how were these policies coordinated? As a practical matter, Europe took its lead from Germany.

The German hegemony

In the early 1980s Europe, like the United States, was suffering from serious inflation. All of the major countries had made fighting inflation a priority. Germany had, however, the best reputation as a diligent inflation-fighter. The German central bank, the Bundesbank, has more independence than its counterparts in France, Italy, and the United Kingdom. Also, the hyperinflation of 1920–23 remains a strong German memory. So Germany was known to be willing to pay the price of fighting inflation.

In this situation the European Monetary System was very useful to governments whose records on inflation were not as good: it offered an opportunity to hitch a ride on German credibility. By matching German monetary policy and thus pegging the value of the franc to that of the mark, French policymakers could hope to convince bond markets, labor unions, and others that they were really serious about getting inflation under control. The same was true for Italy and eventually for Spain and the United Kingdom; smaller European countries like Denmark and the Netherlands naturally fell into line. In effect, all of Europe voluntarily adopted German monetary leadership as a way of proving its commitment to stable prices.

It's worth pointing out that German leadership was not the result of overwhelming economic dominance. Germany is the largest economy in Europe, but its GDP is only about 25 percent larger than that of France, the next largest, and it accounts for only 28 percent of the GDP of the European Community as a whole. Germany could not have ruled Europe's money if it had not been a big economy—try to imagine a Dutch monetary hegemony—but its leadership was not inevitable.

Nonetheless, the tacit arrangement under which Germany controlled Europe's money worked very well as long as German interests and those of the rest of Europe coincided. From 1982 until 1990, fighting inflation was everyone's main priority, and leadership by the stern Bundesbank was widely accepted.

Then came the big shock: the reunification of West and East Germany in 1989.

German reunification and the breakup of the EMS

When East Germany emerged from communist rule, it turned out that the economy was a mess. Productivity was low, factories were antiquated, and there were huge needs for investment in infrastructure and environmental cleanup. It quickly became apparent that the West German economy would need to start running large budget deficits to pay for the rebuilding of the East.

Now these large budget deficits tended to raise demand in West Germany, which could be inflationary. In order to offset this inflation risk, the Bundesbank raised interest rates—a sensible policy from Germany's point of view.

The rise in German interest rates, however, caused serious problems for the rest of Europe. In order to stay within the EMS, countries like France or the United Kingdom were obliged to match Germany's tight money without getting the benefits of Germany's fiscal stimulus. The paradoxical result was that the cost of Germany's reunification ended up producing a recession, not in Germany, but in the rest of Europe.

The logical answer should have been a realignment of parities, raising the value of the mark in terms of other European currencies. But policymakers, who had heavily invested their credibility in the defense of stable exchange rates, were reluctant to contemplate such a realignment. From 1990 until September of 1992, Europe more or less drifted, hoping that the strains on the system would somehow go away.

Finally the system cracked. As the recession in the United Kingdom deepened, political pressure on that country's government increased. Speculators, guessing that the pound might be devalued, began pulling money out of the United Kingdom, forcing the British government to spend huge sums trying to maintain its currency's value. After spending $30 billion in a few days, the British gave up on September 17, dropping out of the EMS and allowing the pound to float. Italy did the same, and several other European countries were forced to devalue.

Interestingly but predictably, the breakup of the EMS immediately reduced the effective linkage among the European economies. By the summer of 1993 the United Kingdom was well on the way to recovery, while France and for that matter Germany itself was slipping deeper into recession.

Lessons for the United States

The United States has been a largely disinterested bystander to European monetary affairs. But what do we learn from the events?

First, the contrasts between the situation within Europe and the situation in the world economy as a whole are a reminder of the limits to international policy coordination. Europe and Japan will not, for the forseeable future, be as important to the U.S. economy as European nations are to each other.

Second, we see that even within Europe the strong interdependence of the last few years had more to do with politics—the commitment to stabilize exchange rates against the mark—than with any economic logic that forced European economies to move in lockstep. Again, it is hard to see any parallel at a global level.

The subject of global finance is fascinating, and it holds a strong attraction for economic pundits and policymakers alike. The bottom line for the United States is, however, that it is surprisingly irrelevant to our domestic problems.

V

American Prospects

Americans no longer expect much from their economy or from the politicians who manage it. They appear to be satisfied so long as disaster is avoided and most people's living standards do not decline. And the most likely forecast for the next decade or so is that Americans will get what they expect—no disaster, but not much good news, either.

Nonetheless, there are other possibilities. Anyone who confidently predicts what the next decade will be like is either foolish or dishonest, for if we learn anything from recent history it is how completely wrong expectations can be. In 1947 most economists were pessimists, expecting the return of mass unemployment. The extraordinary growth of the next 25 years surprised them all. In the early 1970s, by contrast, nearly everyone was excessively optimistic. None of the major economic difficulties of the 1970s and 1980s—the energy crisis, the productivity slowdown, the rise of European unemployment, the debt crisis—was foreseen. So history teaches us to be humble and to entertain a variety of possibilities.

The final part of this book sketches out three scenarios. In the first scenario everything works out just fine. In the second, impatience with the economy's sluggish performance leads to policies based on wishful thinking, precipitating a major economic crisis sometime during the next decade. Finally, the third scenario is one in which we simply drift along, experiencing neither disaster nor striking success—until the demographics begin to catch up with us.

Three points should be emphasized about these scenarios. First, they represent an attempt to stay within the range of the plausible. Something wonderful or terrible could always happen—cold fusion could turn out to work, or the spread of AIDS could turn into a crippling burden. The scenarios presented here, however, are all based on relatively reasonable assumptions.

Second, these are scenarios, not forecasts. Looking back from the year 2017, we will surely marvel at our stupidity in 1997. We will wonder how we could have failed to notice these developments that would be crucial in the years ahead (spectacular economic growth in liberalized Eastern Europe and Russia? a super savings and loan crisis as other hidden government liabilities come to light?) In short, these scenarios are illustrations of the kinds of things that might happen, not predictions of what will happen.

Finally, there is a fourth scenario that I do not include. This is the scenario in which the voters and the politicians take a realistic view of the situation, and decide to act responsibly and decisively now rather than wait until action becomes unavoidable. It is easy to describe the economics of this scenario, but it seems so unlikely that it is hardly worth discussing.

15

Happy Ending

The race is not to the swift, nor the battle to the strong, neither yet bread to the wise, nor yet flourishing economies to policymakers of understanding. It is perfectly possible that the American economy will, over the next decade, deliver a level of performance that will make our current anxieties look foolish and perhaps persuade our leaders that they were somehow responsible.

The key is productivity. If productivity growth in the United States were to recover to something like its rates of the 1950s and 1960s, practically everything would fall into place.

A productivity revival?

It's not too hard to make a case that productivity growth in the next decade will be much better than it was in the last two. In fact, there are at least four schools of productivity optimists: statistical, generational, managerial, and technological.

The statistical case for a productivity revival starts from the one sure fact in all of this: We don't know much about why productivity growth varies. In particular, we really don't know why productivity grew rapidly from 1945 to 1973, then very slowly thereafter. Since we don't know why growth slowed, we cannot confidently argue that it might not speed up again.

The history of U.S. productivity growth in the twentieth century can be read as encouraging. Looking back at the 10-year average rates of productivity growth shown in Figure 6, we see that this rate has fluctuated around 2 percent, sometimes more, sometimes less. Never mind why: Suppose that it turns out that the 1950s and 1960s were just a lucky draw, and the 1970s and 1980s a bad one. There is no reason that the next decade shouldn't be another good draw, with productivity growth above 2 percent—and perhaps as high as 3 percent. Judging from the figure, that's well within the range of the possible.

The technological argument for a productivity revival occurs to almost anyone who reads the "science and technology" section of his favorite business magazine. Technologically, the past 15 years have been a parade of wonders: Especially in computation, but also in communication (remember life before the fax?), there has been one revolution after another, with new areas such as biotechnology now seemingly on the verge of widespread practical implementation. Yet economically, the news has been generally dreary—a typical American worker can buy less with his pay today than his father could when Richard Nixon was first inaugurated.

Something is out of kilter here. Either technology isn't all it's cracked up to be, or we haven't yet seen the impact of the new technology on our economy. Maybe the next decade will see businesses learn how to use computers, fiberoptics, and the Internet to do something really useful, and the rate of growth will pick up. The highest rate of U.S. productivity growth before the 1950s was in the 1920s, driven by the automobile industry—even though automobiles had been in existence and even in fairly widespread use since the turn of the century. We are arguably in the same situation with regard to personal computers: They are around, but only now are we about to use them creatively to transform our lives.

The managerial argument for rapid growth rests on a peculiar dissonance between what business leaders think they are accomplishing and what the statistics say they have achieved. Ask the top executives of almost any company about productivity and they will tell you that in the last few years their industry has made great strides—that new technologies, new work discipline, an emphasis on quality, and the painful removal of excess staff through downsizing have produced a "productivity revolution." To borrow a British campaign slogan, business insists that it hurt, but it worked. But the actual productivity numbers do not show any acceleration. Business leaders maintain that the numbers are wrong—or perhaps they reflect some temporary adjustment costs in the process of transforming the economy. Any day now, they assure, it will become clear just how rapidly productivity is now increasing.

Lastly, the generational argument for accelerating growth simply points out that the 1960s are receding into the past. If you think that the ultimate source of the productivity problem lay in the fact that too many talented people dropped out, wasted years trying to become social workers, and/or avoided entrepreneurial or corporate careers because of misplaced idealism, then you would expect to see faster growth as the success-oriented post–baby-boom generation makes its way up the ladder.

None of these arguments is conclusive. In particular, it is possible to make a compelling case that America's social problems—the growth of the underclass, and the decline of educational quality and achievement even among middle-class children—will drag down our productivity growth even further. But the truth is that nobody knows.

If the optimists are right, and productivity growth does accelerate, when will the good news start to come in? That is an interesting story, worth a brief digression.

The productivity revolution: now or never?

A funny thing happened to the U.S. economy on the way to the 1992 election. By one criterion—growth of output—an economic recovery began in the middle of 1991. But that recovery initially created hardly any new jobs, and in fact the unemployment rate continued to rise. From the point of view of most people, a "jobless recovery" is basically no recovery at all, and public frustration had a lot to do with the defeat of the incumbent president.

But why didn't output growth translate into employment growth? Although it was a fairly sluggish recovery by historical standards, the main reason was a jump in productivity. Indeed, productivity grew 3.4 percent in 1992, its best performance since 1976. This was initially bad news for the administration and for unemployed workers, but it led many economists to conclude that the country had finally put the productivity slowdown behind it. The new determination of management, plus the application of new technologies, were finally paying off in a return of rapid growth.

There were a few dissenters. In particular, Robert Gordon of Northwestern University cautioned strongly that this productivity surge might reflect no more than the business cycle. He pointed out that during the fairly shallow recession of 1990–91, firms had been slow to lay off workers. Based on this fact, plus historical evidence on productivity shifts over the cycle, he suggested that most of the productivity surge was a one-time event: because companies had held on to workers when output was declining, they could now increase production up to a point without hiring new workers. But once the excess labor had been brought into use, the productivity surge would fade out.

Gordon was right. After growing rapidly for a year and a half, productivity growth slowed back to rates of 1 percent per year or less. Announcements of a productivity revolution were, it turned out, premature.

The interesting thing was that as new data began to show that a productivity revolution was not in progress after all, a significant number of people refused to believe the data. They were sure, based on their own sense of what was actually happening, that productivity really *was* surging, and could only conclude that the numbers were wrong. They became even more convinced of this when the Bureau of Economic Analysis, which produces productivity statistics, made a technical revision in its procedures that reduced the rate of estimated productivity growth, which had initially seemed at least somewhat faster than in the 1980s, to levels that approached historic lows. This wasn't the American economy they thought they saw.

How could the productivity statistics be wrong? The main answer is that it is difficult for statistics to capture fundamental changes in technology or quality. How do you measure the "output" generated by the widespread replacement of telephone and mail communication by electronic mail? The productivity optimists insist that a productivity revolution has already begun, but is invisible because our economic statistics are out of date in a world of fundamental technological progress.

Most economists, however, believe that the statistics do not greatly understate productivity growth. One reason is that if productivity really is growing very fast, there is a puzzle about the accounting: real incomes do not seem to be rising rapidly, so where is the higher output going? Also, while there have been some impressive technological advances in recent years, there is a real question about whether they are really all that fundamental in terms of their impact on the economy. The Internet is a lot of fun, and very useful to some people; but think back to the advances that drove the sustained productivity boom from the 1940s to the 1970s. During the postwar generation car ownership, home refrigerators, supermarkets, passenger air travel (the Boeing 747 was introduced in 1969), and direct-dial long-distance calling created a true revolution in the way people lived and worked. Have any of the recent achievements, however impressive, made a comparable difference?

In short, there is a deep divide in opinion. Technological optimists think that a productivity boom may not even be around the corner—it is already here. Pessimists think that the technologies that will supposedly drive the boom have been overhyped, and that no relief is in prospect.

The consequences of a productivity boom

Suppose that the optimists turn out to be right, and that U.S. productivity grows much faster in the decade ahead than it did in the past 15 years—say, at close to 3 percent a year. How would this affect the economy?

The answer is that it would make many, but not all, of the problems discussed in this book fade away.

To begin with, rapid productivity growth would lead to a general rise in living standards. If productivity were to grow as fast in the decade ahead as it did in the 1960s, the average American worker's take-home pay would grow by something like 30 percent. Unless there were an extraordinary further increase in inequality, this growth in income would be widely shared. As a result, the era of growing misery at the bottom of the income scale would be over.

Faster productivity growth would also do a great deal to defuse the problem of the trade deficit through a variety of indirect channels. First, faster growth would raise tax revenues. While some demands on the public purse would also grow more rapidly (like demands for increased infrastructure investment), others—notably defense and interest on the public debt—would not. So the budget deficit would fade away, and as a consequence the national savings rate would rise, contributing to a decline in the trade deficit.

At the same time, faster growth would minimize the consequences of trade deficits. While claims of foreigners on the U.S. economy would continue to rise (at least for a while), they would be a smaller piece of a larger pie and would thus create less of a drain. And a U.S. economy that was doing relatively well would probably experience less conflict with Japan, even if Japan were doing still better.

Faster productivity growth would not, of course, solve every economic problem, and it may be useful to remind ourselves of what it would not do. It would not necessarily reduce the unemployment rate: America did very well at containing unemployment during the 1970s and 1980s, despite low productivity growth, while Europe did badly, despite substantially faster productivity growth. It would not necessarily help reduce inflation: Inflation in the U.S. first took off in the high-growth 1960s and was brought largely under control in the low-growth 1980s. It would not even protect the economy from the risks of financial crisis: Both the 1929 crash and the 1982 Latin American debt crisis followed decades of unusually high productivity growth in their victims.

Still, it is important to realize that a spontaneous productivity revival that would not be out of line with past experience could solve most of the pressing economic issues facing the United States without any positive action from our leadership. We could simply get lucky. On a purely unscientific basis, I would assign this kind of happy ending a probability of 20 percent.

Despite the general contentment of the American public with their country's economic performance, predictions of catastrophe—doomsday books—still do a brisk business. While most of these predictions (the ones that sell best) are pure fantasy, there is a widespread undercurrent of concern that somehow the excesses of the 1980s—the budget deficit, the trade deficit, the growth of corporate debt—have prepared the ground for a future crisis.

Where might such a crisis come from? Popular books on economic crisis usually draw their images from 1929: a collapse of business confidence leading to global financial collapse. But a 1929-style crisis is quite unlikely in the modern world, for reasons to be discussed in a moment. A better bet is a crisis arising either from over-optimistic monetary expansion or from fiscal mismanagment.

1929 again?

The image of 1929 still haunts many Americans: the bubble of optimism suddenly bursts, stockbrokers leap from windows, prosperity vanishes almost overnight. Can it happen again?

It depends on what you mean. Can a stock market crash like that of 1929 happen again? Yes, of course it can—in fact, it already has. The initial fall in U.S. stock prices in the 1987 crash was as large as that of 1929, and the collapse spread around the world faster and more thoroughly. Could such a crash generate another depression? No. It didn't in 1987, and it almost surely won't the next time it happens.

By purely financial measures, the crash of 1987 was every bit as bad as the initial financial panic in 1929. The initial fall in the U.S. stock prices was slightly larger in 1929; but in 1987 the U.S. fall was much more nearly matched by the decline abroad. So on a global basis Black Monday in 1987 was actually worse than Black Thursday in 1929.

But from that point on the stories diverge totally. The initial crash in 1929 was followed by a deepening recession and by successive waves of further stock decline. The 1987 crash was followed by relatively rapid economic growth and a corresponding recovery of stock prices that soon erased virtually all of the initial drop.

Why didn't 1987 play like 1929? The basic answer is a surprising one, given today's widespread cynicism about economic policy and the role of government: We've learned something since 1929, and the Federal Reserve used that knowledge effectively. Stock market crashes need not cause severe downturns in the real economy. The crash in 1929 helped intensify a recession that was already developing. Even a year later that recession seemed unpleasant, but not menacing. What really turned the crash into the Depression was the collapse of the banking system in 1931, which led to a huge contraction in the availability of credit. In the judgment of most of those who have studied the events, this banking collapse was simply unnecessary. It happened only because of the almost eerie passivity of the Federal Reserve, which failed to do anything to stop it, permitting massive deflation and monetary collapse in the early 1930s.

In 1987 the Federal Reserve chose not to repeat its previous mistake. Faced with the stock crash, it rapidly expanded the supply of base money. The rest is already history. Instead of a Depression, there was faster growth in the year following the crash than in the year before. Indeed, the 1987 crash may actually have improved the economy's performance by leading to a rise in the personal savings rate. The Fed demonstrated that it is not only possible but easy to insulate the real economy from a financial panic.

Of course a misguided or incompetent Federal Reserve could still manage to turn some future stock crash into something serious. On a true gold standard, for example, or with a rigid monetarist rule in effect, the Federal Reserve would have been unable to carry out the rapid credit expansion of late 1987. Given reasonably competent and flexible management, however, there does not seem to be any reason to expect a repeat of 1929.

A crisis of over-optimism

One of the peculiarities of the popular debate over U.S. economic policy in the mid-1990s was the emergence of a sort of coalition of the left and right against the center on the issue of monetary policy. Both tax-cutting conservatives, like the editor of the *Wall Street Journal* (who did more than anyone else to promote the economic theory that led to Reagan's tax cuts—and the emergence of massive deficits) and big-spending liberals, like financier Felix Rohatyn (who argued through much of the 1980s and 1990s that America needed a massive dose of New Deal-type public works programs) agreed that the Federal Reserve was setting far too low a target for economic growth. That is, both groups agreed that the Fed could print much more money without creating inflation, and that if it would only loosen up, there would be room to cut taxes or increase spending.

Most economists thought that this "growthism," at least in the extreme form that called for a growth target of 3.5 or even 4 percent for many years, was simply silly. Statistical evidence suggested strongly that every extra percentage point of growth over about 2.3 percent would lower the unemployment rate by about half a percentage point; since the unemployment rate was only a bit over 5 percent in 1996, to achieve 4 percent growth over a period of six or seven years would require a negative unemployment rate at the end. More to the point, while there might be some dispute about the precise value of the NAIRU, even two years of rapid growth would push the economy into a range that all estimates indicated was highly inflationary.

Although growthism had few adherents among professional economists, it commanded widespread support among journalists and politicians. Influential publications like The *Wall Street Journal, Business Week,* and *U.S. News and World Report* hammered away at the Fed, demanding faster growth. And President Bill Clinton even tried to appoint Felix Rohatyn as vice chairman of the Fed (but Congress blocked him because of his liberalism). The power of growthism reflected, above all, the desire to square the circle: the desire to achieve a balanced budget, cut taxes, and spend more money on some things without making politically painful cuts elsewhere.

Because growthism met this need, there remains a real possibility that sometime over the next decade Congress and the administration will demand that the Fed adopt an unrealistically high growth target. We can predict the consequences fairly easily, not only from economic theory but also from the prior experience of other countries, especially the United Kingdom.

The United Kingdom had its own version of growthism in the mid-1980s. Between 1979 and 1985, the government of Margaret Thatcher had carried out a draconian economic policy, crushing the power of labor unions and bringing inflation down from

nearly 20 to less than 4 percent. Despite reforms that were supposed to make markets work better, however, unemployment
remained extremely high at almost 12 percent. Thatcherites felt
that it must surely be time for a payoff. The Bank of England does
not have the same kind of autonomy the Fed has: it is simply an
arm of the British Treasury, and obeys political instructions. So
when a consumer boom developed in Britain after 1985, the Bank
of England simply stood aside and let the economy grow.

The initial results were exhilarating. Unemployment fell rapidly, dropping below 7 percent in 1989. Thatcherites proclaimed the
triumph of their policies. But as the boom progressed, inflation
began to accelerate, eventually rising above the psychologically
crucial 10 percent level. Faced with the return of double-digit
inflation, the Bank of England had no choice but to slam on the
brakes. From 1990 to 1992 Britain entered a severe recession that
drove the unemployment rate back above 10 percent.

One obvious possibility for a crisis, then, is a U.S. repeat of that
performance. Suppose that sometime in the late 1990s the Fed is
bullied into a grossly over-optimistic policy of expansion. For two
or three years, the result might indeed be rapid growth; then as
inflation began to rocket upward, policy would reverse, and there
would be a severe recession, perhaps as severe as the 1979–82
slump.

There is also, of course, the possibility that even given the
warning signs policy would not reverse—that the United States
could manage to have a *really* serious inflation, Latin American
style, reaching hundreds or even thousands of percent per year.
But that can't happen here—can it?

A government debt crisis

While the deficits and debt of the U. S. government are very high
given the absence of any recent major war, the budget picture

right now is not serious enough to cause any big problems under normal circumstances. While many economists are deeply worried about the long-term fiscal health of the federal government, those worries center on the period after 2010 when the retiring baby boomers will place massive demands on Social Security and Medicare. Still, a government debt crisis could be arranged in the next decade if we try hard enough.

To have a debt crisis, the first thing that would have to happen is a considerable reduction in the *maturity* of government debt—the number of years until repayment of the typical bond. Consider two extremes. At one extreme the government could issue consols: bonds that pay interest every year forever. In that case the government would issue new bonds only to the extent it needed to finance a deficit—annual government borrowing would simply be equal to the budget deficit. At the other extreme, suppose that government debt consisted entirely of very short-term notes, say one-month Treasury bills. Then every month the government would have to pay off its whole debt, which it would normally do by "rolling over" the debt, issuing new Treasury bills equal in value to those expiring plus any additional borrowing needed to finance the deficit.

The average maturity of government debt is currently quite long: about five and a half years. However, there have been times when that maturity has been much shorter: in the late 1970s it was less than three years. And in other countries the maturity of debt has become shorter still. Indeed, in Brazil in the early 1990s much of the debt actually consisted of one-day loans, which had to be repaid every 24 hours!

The main reason why the maturity of government debt sometimes becomes short is uncertainty about inflation. When investors worry about the possibility of a drastic acceleration of inflation, they are unwilling to commit themselves to a long-term loan fixed in money terms. They will do so for a sufficient prices, of course; but governments typically respond to the desires of investors by shifting to shorter maturity debt. That is why the maturity of U.S. debt was so much shorter in the high-inflation 1970s than it is in the low-inflation 1990s. If we once again have a bout of inflation—perhaps because of a period in which "growthists" get their way—the maturity could become short once again.

But why is that a problem? Because a government with a lot of short-term debt is vulnerable to crises of investor confidence.

Suppose, for example, that by 2002 the U.S. government, while hardly deeper in debt relative to GDP than it is now, has shifted to financing a large fraction of its debt with three-month Treasury bills. And suppose that for whatever reason private investors become nervous about the safety of that debt. For example, they might fear that inflation was accelerating out of control; or that the dollar would fall sharply in value against other currencies; or even that the United States would for some reason fail to pay its bills on time, perhaps because of a conflict between Congress and the president. The important point is that if the government has a sufficiently large amount of short-term debt, such a loss of confidence can easily turn into a self-fulfilling prophecy.

The reason is that if investors become unwilling to lend money to the government, unwilling to roll over the existing debt, the government finds itself in an impossible financial position: it simply does not have the cash to pay all of the debt coming due. And that means that even if the government was not originally planning to stop payment, even if its finances are "fundamentally sound," the fear of the market that it might be in trouble can create a crisis that justifies those fears.

Like all of our crisis scenarios, this one has precedents. When Mexico plunged into crisis at the end of 1994, its fiscal situation did not look particularly troubled—but it was heavily reliant on short-term debt. The abrupt loss of investor confidence created a crisis that made investors' fears look entirely reasonable. In short, once a government has become heavily reliant on short-term debt, it may be vulnerable to fiscal crisis even if it does not seem to have any deep-seated problem of solvency.

It is hard to imagine the U. S. government getting into that position, especially because current policymakers at the Fed and Treasury are very aware of the danger. To get into that kind of crisis would require that the better judgment of experienced officials be completely overriden, and that the market shake off a long tradition of regarding the obligations of the U.S. government as the safest assets there are. It is unlikely—but possible.

The truth is that while crises happen, the big problem facing the U. S. economy is probably not the risk that a crisis will shatter our prosperity during the next decade. The odds are that we will instead manage more or less acceptably, and that our policy in this age of diminished expectations will simply be one of drift.

17   Drift

This final scenario is the one that comes closest to a forecast. It describes an American economy in which the next decade or so is much like the last few years: in which there are no radical developments, either favorable or unfavorable, that make the economy of the next ten years very different from that of the last ten. In this scenario economic policy continues much as it has, with no major departures.

There are some countries for which this kind of scenario would be patently absurd—in which one can look at evaporating foreign exchange reserves or spiraling inflation and declare that either a massive change in policies or a slide into anarchy must occur within a few months. The United States is not in that kind of situation (not yet, anyway). There is nothing in the basic arithmetic of U. S. budget deficits, foreign debt, or inflation that would prevent us from continuing more or less with current policies for another decade.

So let us suppose that the United States manages to drift along with no radical departures. What might the economy look like?

A decade of drift

The most likely forecast for the U. S. domestic economy in the next decade is that it will look a lot like 1995–96: fairly slow growth, modestly rising incomes for most Americans, generally good employment performance, some inflation but not enough to cause real problems.

If productivity growth does not accelerate, U.S. economic growth will actually be slower in the next decade than it was in the 1970s and 1980s. The reason is demographic: The baby boomers are all now in the work force, and the great increase in female participation seems to have reached its limits. So in this central scenario we would see the U. S. economy grow only a bit more than 2 percent in an average year.

Median family income, however, would probably do a little better than in the last 20 years, partly because the number of families will not grow as fast, and partly because there are some signs that the growth in income inequality is starting to level off. So the typical family might gain as much as 10 percent in income over the course of the decade. If, as recent data suggest, the widening of the gap between highly skilled and less skilled workers has also slowed, the next decade will differ from the previous 15 years in showing some rise in income for many of the poor. At the very bottom, however, everything we know points to a growing and ever more miserable underclass, its misery aggravated by cuts in social programs; the number of truly desperate poor will grow, as will the associated social pathologies. In other words, the middle class will probably do better in the 1990s than in the 1980s, but the ugly contrast between great affluence for one minority and intense poverty for another should be even greater in the year 2006.

Meanwhile, unemployment and inflation will probably stay fairly low. Admittedly, the Federal Reserve is under pressure from both sides. Some critics want it to make a determined drive for zero inflation, which would (as we have seen) impose a high if temporary cost in unemployment. Others (as we have also seen) want it to adopt ambitious targets for economic growth, which would lead to a revival of inflation. But the Fed at this point seems unmoved by both sets of critics, and nobody seems about to pressure it into acting in a way that it does not want to.

What about the two deficits—trade and budget?

The answer is that both will probably persist, but will not create any crisis. In 1996 the budget deficit was less than 2 percent of GDP. This meant that the federal government's debt was growing at about 3 percent per year—less than the growth rate of nominal GDP, so that the ratio of debt to GDP was actually declining. What happens over the next decade depends on whether you believe the promises of politicians to balance the budget by the early years of the next century, or forecasts that say that without major and politically unpopular steps to cut spending or raise taxes, the budget deficit will soon start to rise again. What is clear, however, is that even if the cynics are right, the ratio of debt to GDP will rise only slowly for most of the next decade. And if you use that ratio to measure the government's fiscal health—as many economists do—there will be little obvious reason for concern.

The arithmetic for the trade deficit is a little different. The United States is continuing to buy more from the rest of the world than it sells in return, and as a result the rest of the world's claims on us are growing more rapidly than our claims on them The rate of increase of our foreign debt, unlike that of government debt, is quite a lot faster than the growth of GDP; so the U.S. economy is, however you look at it, going deeper into debt to the rest of the world. Despite many years of trade deficits, however, the United States is still far less heavily in debt to foreigners as a share of GDP than most countries that have experienced debt crises. Once again, the huge size of the U.S. economy makes raw comparisons of dollar figures irrelevant: the United States can carry a trillion dollars of debt far more easily than, say, Mexico can carry its mere $100 billion.

So the United States could, quite possibly, get away with no serious change in economic policies for the next decade.

Looking back at the future

To many Americans this scenario will sound reasonably good. There is no crisis; most people are better off. If the economy actually delivers fairly steady growth at more than 2 percent for the next decade, if inflation remains in single digits, if unemployment stays at roughly current levels, most people will count the decade a success. There will doubtless be caustic remarks from politicians and journalists about the foolishness of those doomsayers who claimed that the trade and budget deficits would bring catastrophe.

Yet this is a scenario that falls far short of what used to be regarded as successful performance. Twenty-five years ago, it was taken for granted that the rapid productivity growth of the postwar period, and corresponding growth in living standards, would continue. When Herman Kahn and associates examined the prospects for the U.S. economy in their 1967 book *The Year 2000*, their most pessimistic scenario called for 2.5 percent annual productivity growth—and they argued strongly that at least 4 percent was more likely. That same year, in another series of essays on the year 2000, *Fortune* magazine projected that real wages by then would climb by 150 percent.

Imagine confronting these forecasters with a nation where productivity increased little more than 1 percent a year, where real hourly wages fell through the 1970s and 1980s, where poverty grew in absolute terms. They would have regarded such an outcome as a highly implausible disaster. They would also have predicted a drastic political reaction—especially if one added to the story greatly increased wealth at the top of the income distribution, a declining American position in the world, and growing foreign ownership of U.S. assets.

Yet this scenario now looks perfectly acceptable, and might even be regarded as a success. What is truly remarkable about our times is that the political system accepts our reduced prospects with so much equanimity.

The end game

While U.S. economic policy could quite easily simply drift through the next decade, toward the end of that decade it will become increasingly obvious even to those who would prefer not to think about it that a change in policy has become urgent. This is not a speculative forecast: one thing that we know for sure is that in 2011 people who were born in 1946 will turn 65, and that when they—and the vast ranks of those who were born in the following quarter century—begin to retire the federal budget will begin to move massively into unsustainable deficit. At the time of writing there seemed to be an unwritten rule of American politics saying that "the long run" means seven years: nobody talks about what will happen after that. Perhaps that means that public debate over U.S. economic policy will suddenly become realistic in the year 2004; or perhaps denial and avoidance will prevail even after that. Sometime before 2010, however, the reality of the looming demographic crunch will become obvious to everyone.

What will happen when the burden of the aging population becomes impossible to ignore? It is very hard to come up with any plausible scenario. Will benefits to retired Americans be sharply reduced? Given the strength of the retirees' lobby, that is hard to imagine—and remember that with an aging population retirees will make up an even larger share of the voting public than they do now. Will taxes on working Americans be raised to unprecedented levels to pay for benefits to the elderly? That too sounds politically implausible. Or will the U.S. government, trapped between these two seeming impossibilities, try to square the circle by simply printing the money, and thereby create a disastrous inflation? That seems inconceivable.

Yet unless there is an extraordinary surge in productivity, a surge of which no sign is currently present, one or more of these unthinkable things will happen. We live in an age of diminished expectations, in which the voting public is generally willing to settle for policy drift; but there is an age to come when even that option will no longer be available.

Index